MW01206388

Honorıng the Departed

El Día de Los Muertos

Day of the Dead

By

A. E. Caballero

About the author

A.E.Caballero is a passionate writer and cultural enthusiast with a deep appreciation for the rich tapestry of Mexican traditions and heritage. Caballero has been immersed in the cultural significance and artistic beauty of the Day of the Dead (El Día de los Muertos) from a young age. This profound connection with the tradition has driven Caballero to share its beauty and significance with a global audience.

With a background in cultural anthropology and a love for storytelling, Caballero brings a unique perspective to the celebration of El Día de los Muertos. By delving into the customs, symbolism, and history of the holiday, Caballero's writing illuminates the depths of this tradition that bridges the realms of the living and the deceased.

"Honoring the Departed" is a testament to Caballero's dedication to preserving the authenticity and spirituality of the Day of the Dead while navigating the challenges and controversies faced by the tradition in the modern world. This book is a labor of love, crafted with the aim of sharing the beauty, complexity, and enduring significance of El Día de los Muertos with readers of all backgrounds.

E. Caballero invites you to explore the vibrant and intricate world of the Day of the Dead through the pages of this book and hopes it will inspire a deeper appreciation of this remarkable celebration.

Connect with E. Caballero on social media or through the provided contact information to continue the conversation about El Día de los Muertos and the traditions that honor the departed.

Appreciation

We extend our heartfelt appreciation to you for choosing to explore the vibrant world of the Day of the Dead with us through "Honoring the Departed: El Dia de Los Muertos - Day of the Dead." Your decision to embark on this cultural journey is both an honor and a celebration of the enduring traditions that bridge the realms of the living and the departed.

This book is a labor of love, crafted with the intention of preserving the authenticity, spirituality, and cultural significance of El Día de los Muertos. It is a testament to the beauty and complexity of a tradition that continues to inspire and captivate people around the world.

By choosing to read these pages, you are not only supporting the author but also becoming part of a community that values and appreciates the richness of Mexican heritage and the celebration of life and death. We hope that this book enriches your understanding of the Day of the Dead and inspires a deeper connection to the traditions that honor the departed.

Please feel free to reach out to the author, E. Caballero, to share your thoughts, questions, or insights. Your feedback is invaluable, and we look forward to hearing from you as you embark on this cultural exploration.

Thank you for your trust and enthusiasm. We hope you find "Honoring the Departed" to be a meaningful and enlightening journey.

Warm regards,

A.E. Caballero

Copyright

Dedication

This book is dedicated to the memory of our loved ones who have departed, those who have left an indelible mark on our lives and continue to inspire us.

To the souls who illuminate our paths and remind us that life is a beautiful tapestry woven from both joy and sorrow, we honor you on these pages.

May your memory be a source of comfort, joy, and connection as we celebrate the enduring traditions of the Day of the Dead.

With love and remembrance,

A.E. Caballero

Table of contents

Day of the dead

How the celebration has evolved over time

Influence of tourism and globalization

Controversies and challenges faced by the tradition

Introduction

In the quiet streets of Mexico and in the heart of Mexican communities around the world, there is a time when death is not feared but celebrated, a moment when the veil between the living and the departed is at its thinnest. This is the Day of the Dead, or "Día de los Muertos," a centuries-old tradition that pays homage to those who have journeyed beyond this world, a time to remember, honor, and rejoice in the lives of loved ones who are no longer with us.

In the following pages, we will embark on a journey into the heart and soul of this vibrant and deeply spiritual celebration. We will explore the historical origins of the Day of the Dead, tracing its roots back to pre-Columbian Mesoamerican cultures and its evolution through the lens of Spanish colonization. We will delve into the cultural significance of this unique ritual, understanding the rich symbolism, regional variations, and the profound role it plays in Mexican culture.

The heart of this celebration is the "ofrenda," an intricate and beautiful altar, adorned with offerings of food, marigolds, sugar skulls, and cherished mementos. We'll learn how to construct a traditional ofrenda and discover the personal stories and experiences that make each one unique.

The culinary traditions of this day are as rich and flavorful as the culture itself. We'll explore the significance of traditional dishes, the role of sugar skulls and pan de muerto, and even provide you with recipes to create these culinary delights in your own home.

Art, music, and dance are essential components of the Day of the Dead, and we'll take a closer look at how artistic expression, from sugar skull decorations to the intricate papel picado, embodies the spirit of the celebration. The sounds and movements of this day will also come to life as we explore the music and dance that are integral to the experience.

Throughout the book, we'll hear the voices of those who celebrate the Day of the Dead, sharing their personal stories and experiences. These narratives will remind us that this is not merely a holiday but a powerful connection to the past and a celebration of life, love, and remembrance.

As we journey through the chapters, we'll uncover the ancient roots and traditions that continue to thrive in the modern world. We'll also address the challenges and controversies that have emerged as this once-local tradition has garnered global attention and how it remains resilient in the face of change.

With each page, we invite you to embrace the Day of the Dead, to learn, to appreciate, and to celebrate. This book is not just an exploration; it's a journey of remembrance and connection. It's a testament to the beauty of a tradition that teaches us that death is not an end but a continuation, a transition to be celebrated with joy, love, and respect.

Join us on this voyage into the heart of the Day of the Dead, and may it inspire you to honor and cherish your own departed loved ones in a profound and beautiful way.

Chapter One: Definition and significance of the Day of the Dead

The Day of the Dead, or "Día de los Muertos" in Spanish, is a vibrant and deeply symbolic Mexican holiday celebrated on November 1st and 2nd. It is a time when families and communities come together to remember and honor their deceased loved ones. This celebration is marked by a rich tapestry of traditions, each carrying profound meaning and significance.

Definition:

At its core, the Day of the Dead is a spiritual and cultural celebration that acknowledges the cycle of life and death. It is not a day of mourning but rather a joyous and colorful commemoration of the deceased. During this time, it is believed that the souls of the departed return to the world of the living to be reunited with their families. The living prepare elaborate ofrendas (altars) laden with offerings, decorate graves, and participate in various customs to welcome and celebrate the presence of these returning souls.

Significance:

- ## Honoring Ancestry:

The Day of the Dead is a way for families to pay their respects to deceased relatives, preserving their memory and continuing the connection with their ancestors. It reinforces the idea that the departed remain an integral part of the family's life.

- ## Spiritual Beliefs:

It reflects the fusion of indigenous Mesoamerican beliefs, particularly the Aztec festival dedicated to the goddess Mictecacihuatl, and Spanish Catholicism, as it is celebrated in close proximity to All Saints' Day and All Souls' Day. This combination of traditions creates a unique and syncretic cultural experience.

- **Symbolism:**

The holiday is rife with symbolism. The ofrenda, for example, is filled with items that hold special significance, such as marigold flowers (cempasúchil) to guide the spirits, sugar skulls (calaveras de azúcar) to represent the deceased, and candles to illuminate their path. The altars and their components all convey a deeper narrative of remembrance and respect.

- **Community and Togetherness:**

The Day of the Dead is a communal celebration, bringing people together to construct ofrendas, visit cemeteries, and share stories and food. It reinforces the importance of family and community bonds.

- **Artistic Expression:**

The holiday is an opportunity for artistic expression through the creation of intricate sugar skulls, papel picado (cut paper), and other crafts. This artistic aspect is not only visually stunning but also serves as a means of personal and communal expression.

- **Celebration of Life:**

Most importantly, the Day of the Dead is a celebration of life itself. It reminds us that death is not the end but a continuation of the journey, a transition to be embraced with joy, love, and respect. It helps people confront mortality in a positive and affirming way.

In summary, the Day of the Dead is a celebration deeply embedded in Mexican culture and spirituality. It offers a unique perspective on the relationship between the living and the departed, emphasizing the idea that through remembrance, the deceased are never truly gone. It stands as a testament to the resilience of cultural traditions and the enduring connection between generations.

Purpose and scope of the book

The purpose of this book, titled "Honoring the Departed: Exploring the Day of the Dead Ritual," is to provide readers with a comprehensive and insightful exploration of the Day of the Dead, a vibrant and culturally significant celebration. This book aims to achieve the following objectives:

- **Educational Insight:**

To offer readers a deep understanding of the history, significance, and cultural context of the Day of the Dead ritual. This book will serve as an educational resource for those seeking to learn about this unique tradition.

- **Cultural Appreciation:**

To promote a profound appreciation for the richness and beauty of Mexican culture, specifically through the lens of the Day of the Dead. Readers will gain insights into the symbolism, art, food, and music that make this celebration so special.

- **Personal Connection:**

To inspire readers to connect with the celebration on a personal level. Through personal stories, experiences, and insights from those who celebrate, the book aims to encourage readers to embrace the spirit of remembrance and celebration in their own lives.

- **Preservation of Tradition:**

To contribute to the preservation of this traditional celebration by documenting its various aspects, explaining its importance, and highlighting the challenges it faces in a changing world.

Scope:

The scope of this book is broad and comprehensive, aiming to cover a wide range of topics related to the Day of the Dead ritual. It encompasses the following key areas:

- **Historical Origins:**

The book delves into the historical roots of the celebration, tracing its origins from pre-Columbian Mesoamerican traditions to its transformation under Spanish influence.

- **Cultural Significance:**

It explores the cultural and spiritual significance of the Day of the Dead, delving into the symbolism, regional variations, and its place within Mexican culture.

- **The Altar (Ofrenda):**

The book provides detailed insights into the construction and significance of the ofrenda, the central element of the celebration.

- **Traditional Foods and Drinks:**

It covers the culinary traditions associated with the Day of the Dead, including traditional dishes, sugar skulls, and pan de muerto, along with recipes for readers to try.

- **Art and Craft:**

Readers will discover the artistic side of the celebration, from sugar skull decorations to papel picado and other traditional crafts.

- **Music and Dance:**

The book explores the role of music and dance in the celebration, including traditional and contemporary forms.

- **The Marigold Path (Cempasúchil):**

It explains the significance of marigolds in the celebration and how they are used to create paths and decorations.

- **Calaveras (Skeletons):**

The book delves into the history and symbolism of calaveras, including literary and artistic representations.

- **Modern Interpretations and Changes:**

Readers will gain insights into how the celebration has evolved over time, the influence of tourism and globalization, and the challenges it faces.

- **Personal Stories and Experiences:**

Through interviews and narratives from individuals who celebrate the Day of the Dead, the book will provide a personal and human touch to the tradition.

In summary, the book's scope is to offer a comprehensive and in-depth exploration of the Day of the Dead ritual, encompassing its history, cultural significance, traditions, art, music, and personal connections. It serves as a guide for readers to understand, appreciate, and embrace this unique celebration of life and remembrance.

Chapter Two: Historical Origins

The historical origins of the Day of the Dead are deeply rooted in the cultural and spiritual traditions of Mexico. This vibrant celebration has evolved over centuries, influenced by a complex interplay of indigenous beliefs and Spanish colonialism. Understanding its historical origins is essential to appreciating the richness of this tradition.

1. Pre-Columbian Mesoamerican Traditions:

The earliest roots of the Day of the Dead can be traced back to indigenous Mesoamerican civilizations, particularly the Aztec, Nahua, and Maya cultures. These civilizations had a profound connection with death and the afterlife. They believed in the cyclical nature of existence and the idea that the dead continued to exist in a parallel realm.

- **Festival of Mictecacihuatl:**

Among the Aztecs, a goddess named Mictecacihuatl was venerated. She presided over the underworld and was a central figure in the observance of death rituals. The festival dedicated to her involved offerings to honor deceased ancestors and appease her.

- **Calavera Traditions:**

These cultures created skull art, such as ceramic and stone skulls, and used them in religious ceremonies and rituals. This laid the foundation for the prominent use of calaveras (skeletons) in the modern Day of the Dead.

2. Spanish Influence:

The arrival of Spanish conquistadors in the 16th century and the subsequent colonization of Mexico brought about a significant transformation in the indigenous death rituals. The Spanish introduced

Catholicism, and the indigenous traditions began to merge with Christian practices.

- **All Saints' Day and All Souls' Day:**

The Catholic Church celebrated All Saints' Day (November 1st) and All Souls' Day (November 2nd) to honor saints and pray for the souls of the deceased. These dates coincided with indigenous rituals, leading to a blending of customs.

- **Altars and Ofrendas:**

The Spanish introduced the concept of creating altars and offering prayers for the deceased. Indigenous people incorporated these practices into their existing traditions, resulting in the creation of ofrendas laden with a mixture of Catholic and indigenous symbols.

3. Evolution into Día de los Muertos:

Over time, these influences gave rise to the modern Day of the Dead, or "Día de los Muertos." The celebration evolved as a unique blend of indigenous, Spanish, and Catholic traditions.

- **Cultural Syncretism:**

Día de los Muertos became a symbol of cultural syncretism, where indigenous beliefs were intertwined with Spanish Catholicism. This syncretic nature continues to be a defining characteristic of the celebration.

- **Regional Variations:**

Different regions of Mexico developed their own variations of the celebration, each with unique customs and practices, often influenced by the local history and indigenous cultures.

Understanding these historical origins provides valuable insights into the Day of the Dead's significance as a celebration of life, death, and the enduring connection between the living and the departed. It showcases the resilience of a tradition that has withstood the test of time, continuing to be a vibrant and cherished part of Mexican culture.

Pre-Columbian Mesoamerican traditions

The roots of the Day of the Dead can be traced back to the rich and complex traditions of indigenous Mesoamerican civilizations that predate the arrival of European colonizers. These traditions laid the foundation for the celebration we know today. Here are some key elements of pre-Columbian Mesoamerican traditions related to death and ancestor veneration:

1. Belief in the Afterlife:

Pre-Columbian Mesoamerican societies, including the Aztecs, Mayans, and Zapotecs, held a profound belief in the afterlife. They believed that life was cyclical, and death was a natural part of this cycle.

They saw death as a transition rather than an end, and they believed that the deceased continued to exist in a different realm.

2. Honoring Ancestors:

Ancestor veneration was a central aspect of pre-Columbian Mesoamerican cultures. Ancestors were revered, and their memory was preserved through various rituals and offerings.

3. Mictecacihuatl and Mictecacihuatlán:

The Aztecs had a goddess named Mictecacihuatl, often referred to as the "Lady of the Dead." She presided over Mictlán, the Aztec underworld.

Mictecacihuatl was a key figure in the Aztec celebration of death and the afterlife. Her festival involved offerings and rituals to honor her and the deceased.

4. Skull Art:

These civilizations created intricate skull art, including ceramic and stone skulls. Skulls were used in religious ceremonies and rituals.

Skulls symbolized death and rebirth, and they were often adorned with colorful designs and patterns.

5. Calaveras (Skeletons):

The concept of calaveras, or skeletons, as symbols of death, transformation, and rebirth, had deep roots in pre-Columbian Mesoamerican cultures.

Calaveras were not just symbols of fear but also of reverence for the cyclical nature of life.

6. Rituals and Offerings:

Various rituals and offerings were made to honor the deceased. These offerings often included food, flowers, incense, and other items believed to nourish the spirits.

7. Ongoing Connection:

The indigenous peoples believed that the deceased continued to play a role in the lives of the living. They saw this connection as an ongoing and integral part of their existence.

The arrival of Spanish colonizers and the spread of Christianity brought about significant changes to these indigenous traditions. Over time, the syncretism of indigenous beliefs with Catholicism led to the evolution of the Day of the Dead, as the Spanish-influenced All Saints' Day and All Souls' Day became intertwined with these pre-Columbian Mesoamerican practices. This merging of cultures created a unique and vibrant celebration of life, death, and the enduring connection between the living and the departed.

Influence of Spanish colonization

The arrival of Spanish colonizers in the 16th century had a profound impact on the indigenous traditions of the Americas, including the indigenous death rituals that would later evolve into the Day of the Dead. Here's an overview of how Spanish colonization influenced the Day of the Dead:

1. Introduction of Catholicism:

One of the most significant influences of Spanish colonization was the introduction of Catholicism. Spanish colonizers were fervent Catholics, and they sought to convert indigenous peoples to Christianity.

2. Syncretism of Beliefs:

The blending of indigenous Mesoamerican beliefs with Catholicism led to the syncretism of religious practices. Indigenous peoples often incorporated Catholic elements into their existing traditions.

This syncretism was particularly evident in the way indigenous death rituals and beliefs merged with Catholic celebrations.

3. All Saints' Day and All Souls' Day:

Spanish Catholicism brought with it the observance of All Saints' Day (Día de Todos los Santos) on November 1st and All Souls' Day (Día de los Fieles Difuntos) on November 2nd.

These Catholic holidays were intended to honor saints and pray for the souls of the deceased. The timing of these holidays coincided with pre-existing indigenous rituals related to the deceased.

4. Altars and Offerings:

Spanish Catholicism emphasized the construction of altars and the offering of prayers for the souls of the departed. This practice was introduced to indigenous communities.

Indigenous peoples incorporated these elements into their own traditions, resulting in the creation of ofrendas (altars) laden with a combination of Catholic and indigenous symbols and offerings.

5. Integration of Symbols:

Spanish and Catholic symbols, such as crosses, religious icons, and images of saints, began to appear alongside indigenous symbols, including calaveras (skeletons) and marigold flowers, in the ofrendas.

6. Cemeteries and Grave Visits:

Spanish colonization also influenced the way indigenous communities cared for the deceased. The concept of burying the deceased in cemeteries, a practice introduced by the Spanish, became more common.

Visits to cemeteries to clean and decorate graves also became part of the tradition, aligning with the European Christian practice of honoring the dead in graveyards.

7. Language and Naming Conventions:

The Spanish language and Catholic naming conventions influenced the way indigenous communities referred to the holiday. "Día de los Muertos," the modern Spanish name for the holiday, was a result of this linguistic influence.

8. Regional Variations:

Spanish colonization and the influence of Catholicism were not uniform across all regions of Mexico. Different regions incorporated these influences to varying degrees, resulting in unique regional variations of the celebration.

The influence of Spanish colonization and the syncretism of beliefs and practices played a pivotal role in shaping the modern Day of the Dead. The celebration we see today is a testament to the resilience of indigenous traditions and their ability to adapt and evolve in the face of external influences, ultimately creating a unique and culturally rich celebration that continues to thrive in Mexico and beyond.

Evolution of the modern celebration

The modern Day of the Dead, or "Día de los Muertos," is a vibrant and culturally significant celebration that has evolved over centuries, merging indigenous Mesoamerican traditions, Spanish colonial influences, and local variations. Here's an overview of the evolution of this celebration:

1. Syncretism of Beliefs:

The arrival of Spanish colonizers in the 16th century introduced Catholicism to the indigenous peoples of Mexico. The syncretism of indigenous beliefs with Catholicism was a significant turning point.

Indigenous practices related to death and ancestor veneration blended with Catholic observances, creating a unique fusion of traditions.

2. All Saints' Day and All Souls' Day:

The Catholic holidays of All Saints' Day on November 1st and All Souls' Day on November 2nd played a pivotal role in the development of the modern celebration.

Indigenous rituals associated with the deceased coincided with these Catholic holidays, leading to the blending of customs and the establishment of specific dates for the celebration.

3. Ofrendas and Altars:

The construction of ofrendas (altars) became a central practice, influenced by Catholic traditions of offering prayers for the deceased.

Ofrendas are now an integral part of the celebration, laden with symbolic offerings such as candles, marigold flowers, incense, sugar skulls, and the favorite foods and possessions of the deceased.

4. Regional Variations:

Different regions of Mexico developed their own unique variations of the celebration. These regional differences are often influenced by local history, indigenous cultures, and even environmental factors.

For example, in some regions, families may light candles and create altars in their homes, while in others, the focus is on visiting cemeteries and decorating graves.

5. Artistic Expression:

The modern celebration is characterized by artistic expression, with colorful and intricate creations such as sugar skulls (calaveras de azúcar) and papel picado (cut paper decorations).

Artistic expressions play a vital role in the visual aspect of the celebration, adding vibrancy and symbolism.

6. Food and Drink:

Traditional foods and drinks associated with the celebration, including pan de muerto (bread of the dead) and mole, have become an essential part of the modern celebration.

These culinary traditions have evolved over time but remain central to the experience.

7. Revival and Globalization:

In the 20th and 21st centuries, there has been a revival of interest in the Day of the Dead, both within Mexico and among Mexican diaspora communities.

The celebration has gained recognition and popularity beyond Mexican borders, with Day of the Dead festivals and events held in various parts of the world.

8. Cultural Resilience:

The Day of the Dead's enduring popularity and cultural significance highlight its resilience in the face of change and globalization. It remains a symbol of Mexican identity and cultural pride.

The modern Day of the Dead is a testament to the adaptability of traditions and the ability of a culture to evolve while maintaining its core principles. It continues to be a celebration of life, death, and the enduring connection between the living and the departed, symbolizing the rich tapestry of Mexican culture and spirituality.

Chapter Three: Cultural Significance

The Day of the Dead, or "Día de los Muertos," is a celebration deeply embedded in Mexican culture. Its cultural significance extends far beyond being a mere holiday, as it touches upon the core values, beliefs, and identity of the Mexican people. Here's an exploration of the cultural significance of this vibrant tradition:

1. Honoring Ancestry:

At its heart, the Day of the Dead is a way for families and communities to honor and remember their ancestors and departed loved ones. This act of remembrance reinforces the importance of family and ancestral ties.

2. Life as a Continuation:

The celebration carries a fundamental belief in the continuity of life beyond death. It emphasizes that the deceased are not gone but continue to exist in another realm, making death a transition to be celebrated rather than feared.

3. Fusion of Traditions:

The Day of the Dead is a living example of cultural syncretism. It represents the fusion of indigenous Mesoamerican traditions, such as Aztec and Maya beliefs, with Spanish Catholicism.

This blending of cultures reflects the history of Mexico and its complex heritage.

4. Symbolism and Tradition:

The holiday is rife with symbolism. Elements such as marigold flowers (cempasúchil), sugar skulls (calaveras de azúcar), and ofrendas (altars) are rich in meaning, serving as visual and sensory representations of remembrance and respect.

5. Regional Variations:

The Day of the Dead showcases the regional diversity within Mexico. Different states and communities have their own unique customs and practices, reflecting their distinct histories and indigenous cultures.

The variation adds to the richness of the tradition, illustrating that it can be deeply personal and communal simultaneously.

6. Community and Connection:

The celebration is a communal event, bringing people together to construct ofrendas, visit cemeteries, and share stories and food. It fosters a sense of community and connection.

It reinforces the idea that people are not alone in their grief; they have the support of their community to remember and celebrate with them.

7. Artistic Expression:

The Day of the Dead is a canvas for artistic expression. From the intricate sugar skull decorations to the delicate papel picado (cut paper) and other crafts, art is woven into the fabric of the celebration.

This artistic aspect serves as both a visual feast and a means of personal and communal expression.

8. Celebration of Life:

Most importantly, the Day of the Dead is a celebration of life itself. It serves as a reminder that life is to be embraced and celebrated, and that death is not an end but a continuation of the journey.

9. Cultural Resilience:

The Day of the Dead has endured for centuries, surviving Spanish colonization and adapting to modern times. Its continued celebration symbolizes cultural resilience and the enduring connection between generations.

In essence, the Day of the Dead is more than a holiday; it is a cultural touchstone that reflects the core values and beliefs of Mexican society. It emphasizes the importance of family, community, remembrance, and a profound connection to both the living and the departed. This celebration is a vibrant tapestry that weaves together the threads of history, spirituality, and the human experience.

Symbolism and meaning of key elements

The Day of the Dead is rich with symbolism, and its various elements carry deep meaning and significance. Each of these elements contributes to the overall narrative of remembrance and celebration. Here are the key elements and their symbolism:

1. Marigold Flowers (Cempasúchil):

Symbolism:

Marigold flowers are often used to create intricate paths and decorations during the celebration. Their vibrant orange and yellow colors are believed to guide the spirits of the deceased to their ofrendas.

Meaning:

Marigolds are a symbol of both life and death. Their bright colors represent the sun, and they are considered a way to light the path for the spirits as they return.

2. Sugar Skulls (Calaveras de Azúcar):

Symbolism:

Sugar skulls, or calaveras de azúcar, are colorful and intricately decorated skull-shaped candies or ornaments. They are used to represent the departed and are often personalized with the names of loved ones.

Meaning:

Sugar skulls are a cheerful and artistic representation of death. They symbolize the celebration of life and the idea that death is not to be feared but embraced with joy and remembrance.

3. Ofrendas (Altars):

Symbolism:

Ofrendas are elaborate altars created to honor the deceased. They are adorned with a variety of offerings, such as candles, incense, food, and mementos.

Meaning:

Ofrendas symbolize the connection between the living and the departed. They provide a physical space for families to remember and celebrate their loved ones, welcoming them back to the world of the living.

4. Pan de Muerto (Bread of the Dead):

Symbolism:

Pan de Muerto is a sweet, round bread with bone-shaped decorations on top. It is a traditional food associated with the celebration.

Meaning:

The bread represents the circle of life and death. The round shape symbolizes the cyclical nature of existence, while the bone-shaped decorations represent the deceased.

5. Incense (Copal):

Symbolism:

Copal incense is commonly used during the celebration. The rising smoke is believed to carry prayers and blessings to the spirit world.

Meaning:

The use of incense symbolizes purification and the spiritual connection between the living and the departed.

6. Candles (Veladoras):

Symbolism:

Candles are an integral part of ofrendas and grave decorations. They are lit to guide the spirits of the deceased and provide illumination for their return.

Meaning:

Candles represent light in the darkness, symbolizing hope and the memory of the departed. Each lit candle signifies a remembrance of a loved one.

7. Papel Picado (Cut Paper Decorations):

Symbolism:

Papel picado consists of intricately cut paper with various designs. It is often used to decorate ofrendas and other spaces during the celebration.

Meaning:

The delicate art of papel picado represents the fragility and beauty of life. The cut paper allows the spirits to pass through the intricate patterns as they return.

8. Favorite Foods and Beverages:

Symbolism:

Families prepare the favorite foods and beverages of the deceased as offerings on ofrendas. These may include traditional dishes, fruits, and even a deceased person's favorite beer or tequila.

Meaning:

These offerings serve to nourish and satisfy the spirits, allowing them to partake in the pleasures they enjoyed in life.

Each of these elements contributes to the visual and sensory tapestry of the Day of the Dead, reinforcing the celebration's central themes of remembrance, connection, and the joyous embrace of life and death.

Regional variations and differences

The Day of the Dead, or "Día de los Muertos," is a celebration with deep cultural roots in Mexico, and it exhibits a remarkable diversity of regional variations and differences. Different states and communities within Mexico have developed their own unique customs and practices, often influenced by local history, indigenous cultures, and environmental factors. Here are some notable regional variations:

1. Oaxaca:

Notable Features:

Oaxaca is renowned for its elaborate and visually stunning celebrations. It is famous for its use of intricately designed sand tapestries called "tapetes," often created on the streets.

Unique Customs:

In Oaxaca, families often decorate ofrendas with carved radishes, known as "radish art" (radicelas). They also have unique culinary traditions, including the preparation of mole and the "pan de yema," a special egg yolk bread.

2. Michoacán:

Notable Features:

In the town of Pátzcuaro, Michoacán, the celebration includes a beautiful tradition of launching candle-lit boats onto Lake Pátzcuaro. The island of Janitzio is particularly famous for this.

Unique Customs:

The people of Michoacán make use of a specific type of marigold known as the "cempasúchil" to create vibrant floral arrangements.

3. Mixtec and Zapotec Regions:

Notable Features:

Indigenous communities in the Mixtec and Zapotec regions of Oaxaca have preserved ancient rituals that differ from the mainstream Day of the Dead celebration.

Unique Customs:

Here, families might construct graveside altars called "nichos" that are distinct from the ofrendas found in other regions.

4. Janitzio, Michoacán:

Notable Features:

Janitzio, an island in Lake Pátzcuaro, has a unique tradition of families spending the night at the gravesites of their loved ones.

Unique Customs:

On the island, fishermen create a tradition of "butterfly fishing," catching the delicate

Monarch butterflies that migrate to the area during the celebration.

5. Xcaret, Quintana Roo:

Notable Features:

In the Yucatán Peninsula, Xcaret, a theme park, hosts a unique Day of the Dead festival. It combines elements of traditional celebration with theatrical performances and art installations.

Unique Customs:

Visitors can witness the "Travesía Sagrada Maya," a reenactment of an ancient Mayan tradition, during the festival.

6. Aguascalientes:

Notable Features:

Aguascalientes, a state in central Mexico, is known for its annual "Festival de las Calaveras" (Festival of Skulls), which includes art exhibitions, parades, and various cultural events.

Unique Customs:

The city hosts a Calaveras parade featuring creative and whimsical calavera sculptures.

7. Chiapas:

Notable Features:

In the Chiapas region, the celebration takes on a unique character influenced by the indigenous cultures of the area.

Unique Customs:

Indigenous communities in Chiapas may incorporate traditional garments and crafts into their Day of the Dead observances.

These are just a few examples of the diverse regional variations in the Day of the Dead celebration in Mexico. The cultural and geographical diversity of the country has led to a tapestry of traditions, each with its own unique customs, artistry, and practices, demonstrating the depth and breadth of this culturally significant celebration.

How the ritual fits into Mexican culture

The Day of the Dead, or "Día de los Muertos," is an integral and deeply ingrained part of Mexican culture. It serves as a unifying thread that weaves together various aspects of Mexican identity, history, and values. Here's how this ritual fits into Mexican culture:

1. Family and Community Bonds:

Mexican culture places a strong emphasis on family and community. The Day of the Dead reinforces these bonds by bringing families and communities together to remember and celebrate their loved ones.

The construction of ofrendas, visits to cemeteries, and shared meals during the celebration foster a sense of togetherness and support.

2. Celebration of Life:

Mexicans have a unique perspective on death, viewing it not as an end but as a continuation of the journey. The Day of the Dead is a joyful celebration of life, a reminder to embrace life's pleasures and not to fear death.

The vibrant colors, lively music, and culinary delights associated with the celebration reflect this celebration of life.

3. Fusion of Indigenous and Spanish Traditions:

Mexican culture is the result of a fusion of indigenous and Spanish traditions. The Day of the Dead epitomizes this syncretism, blending ancient Mesoamerican beliefs with Spanish Catholicism.

This fusion highlights the ability of Mexican culture to adapt and evolve while preserving its rich heritage.

4. Artistic Expression:

Art is a significant part of Mexican culture, and the Day of the Dead is a canvas for artistic expression. From intricate sugar skulls to papel picado, art is deeply integrated into the celebration.

This artistic aspect reflects the creativity and craftsmanship that are valued in Mexican culture.

5. Culinary Traditions:

Mexican cuisine is celebrated worldwide, and the Day of the Dead brings together culinary traditions that are an integral part of Mexican culture.

Traditional foods like pan de muerto, mole, and tamales hold a special place in the celebration, showcasing the diversity of Mexican culinary heritage.

6. Indigenous Heritage:

Mexican culture is rooted in indigenous heritage, and the Day of the Dead allows for the preservation of indigenous traditions and practices.

It serves as a testament to the enduring influence of indigenous cultures in Mexican society.

7. Regional Diversity:

Mexico is a culturally diverse country with distinct regional customs and traditions. The regional variations in the Day of the Dead celebration demonstrate the cultural richness and complexity of Mexico.

Each region's unique approach to the celebration adds depth to the overall cultural tapestry.

8. Cultural Resilience:

The Day of the Dead has endured through centuries of change, including Spanish colonization and modernization. Its continued celebration is a testament to the cultural resilience and preservation of Mexican traditions.

In summary, the Day of the Dead is not just a ritual; it is a cultural cornerstone that reflects the core values and beliefs of Mexican society. It reinforces the importance of family, community, remembrance, and the celebration of life and death. It embodies the creativity, resilience, and enduring spirit of Mexican culture, making it a beloved and integral part of the nation's identity.

Chapter Four: The Altar (Ofrenda)

The centerpiece of the Day of the Dead celebration is the ofrenda, a beautifully crafted and highly symbolic altar dedicated to honoring and welcoming the spirits of the deceased. The ofrenda is a sacred space where families pay tribute to their loved ones and create a bridge between the living and the departed. Here's a closer look at the ofrenda:

1. Purpose of the Ofrenda:

The ofrenda serves as a focal point for the celebration, creating a spiritual connection between the living and the deceased. It is a physical space where families and communities come together to remember, celebrate, and welcome back the souls of their loved ones.

2. Elements of the Ofrenda:

The ofrenda is adorned with a variety of elements, each with its own symbolic meaning:

Marigold Flowers (Cempasúchil):

Marigolds are believed to guide the spirits to the ofrenda with their vibrant colors.

Candles (Veladoras):

Candles represent the light that guides the spirits and also symbolize hope.

Incense (Copal):

The fragrant smoke of copal incense is thought to purify the space and serve as a pathway for prayers to reach the spirits.

Papel Picado:

Elaborately cut paper decorations hang above the ofrenda, representing the fragility of life.

Calaveras (Sugar Skulls):

Sugar skulls are inscribed with the names of the deceased and are a whimsical representation of death.

Favorite Foods and Beverages:

Traditional dishes, fruits, and the favorite foods and drinks of the departed are placed on the ofrenda to nourish the souls.

Water: Water quenches the thirst of the spirits after their journey and is often placed in a container on the ofrenda.

Salt:

Salt represents purification and preservation and is included to purify the souls of the deceased.

Photographs and Mementos:

Pictures and personal mementos of the deceased are placed on the ofrenda to remind the living of their loved ones.

Crosses and Religious Icons:

Catholic elements are sometimes incorporated into the ofrenda, symbolizing the fusion of indigenous and Catholic beliefs.

3. Levels of the Ofrenda:

Ofrendas often have multiple tiers or levels. The top level typically represents the heavens, the middle level represents the earthly realm, and the bottom level symbolizes the underworld. These levels correspond to the journey of the spirits.

4. Personalization:

Ofrendas are highly personalized, reflecting the unique life and preferences of the deceased. The photographs and mementos, along with the inclusion of their favorite foods and possessions, create a deeply personal and emotional connection.

5. Location:

Ofrendas are typically placed in homes, cemeteries, or community spaces. Families may have ofrendas for each of their deceased loved ones.

6. Visiting the Ofrenda:

Families and friends gather around the ofrenda to share stories, prayers, and memories of the deceased. It is a time for reflection, celebration, and communion with the spirits.

The ofrenda is a visual and sensory masterpiece that encapsulates the essence of the Day of the Dead, bridging the realms of the living and the departed. It symbolizes the profound connection between generations and the enduring memory of loved ones, making it one of the most cherished and sacred aspects of the celebration.

Components and their significance

The ofrenda (altar) in the Day of the Dead celebration is a carefully arranged and highly symbolic space that serves as a bridge between the living and the deceased. Each component of the ofrenda carries deep meaning and significance. Here are the key components and their symbolism:

1. Marigold Flowers (Cempasúchil):

Significance: Marigold flowers are believed to guide the spirits of the deceased with their vibrant colors and their strong scent.

Meaning: The marigolds symbolize the sun, and their petals are laid out in intricate paths and patterns to lead the spirits from the world of the living to the ofrenda.

2. Candles (Veladoras):

Significance: Candles represent light, hope, and faith. They guide the spirits back to the world of the living and provide illumination for their return.

Meaning: The light of the candles symbolizes the memory of the departed and serves as a beacon for their souls.

3. Incense (Copal):

Significance: Copal incense is believed to purify the space and is used to create a fragrant pathway for prayers to reach the spirits.

Meaning: The rising smoke represents the spiritual connection between the living and the deceased. It purifies the environment and creates a link to the spirit world.

4. Papel Picado (Cut Paper Decorations):

Significance: Papel picado consists of intricately cut paper decorations that hang above the ofrenda. These paper designs represent the fragility of life.

Meaning: The cut paper allows the spirits to pass through the intricate patterns and is a symbol of life's delicate beauty.

5. Calaveras (Sugar Skulls):

Significance: Sugar skulls are often personalized with the names of the deceased and serve as whimsical representations of death.

Meaning: They symbolize the celebration of life and the idea that death is not to be feared but embraced with joy and remembrance.

6. Favorite Foods and Beverages:

Significance: The ofrenda is laden with the favorite foods and beverages of the deceased. These offerings are meant to nourish the spirits during their visit.

Meaning: The act of preparing and sharing the favorite dishes of the departed shows a deep respect for their memory and a desire to ensure their comfort in the afterlife.

7. Water:

Significance: Water is placed in a container on the ofrenda to quench the thirst of the spirits after their long journey from the spirit world.

Meaning: The water represents life, renewal, and purification, making it essential for the souls to refresh themselves.

8. Salt:

Significance: Salt is included to purify the souls of the deceased and is often placed in a dish on the ofrenda.

Meaning: Salt represents purification and preservation, ensuring that the spirits are cleansed and preserved as they return to the world of the living.

9. Photographs and Mementos:

Significance: Personal photographs and mementos of the deceased are placed on the ofrenda to remind the living of their loved ones and to celebrate their lives.

Meaning: These items keep the memory of the departed alive, providing a visual and emotional connection to their presence.

10. Crosses and Religious Icons:

Significance: In some ofrendas, crosses and religious icons are incorporated, symbolizing the fusion of indigenous and Catholic beliefs.

Meaning: These symbols represent the spiritual journey of the deceased and the connection between earthly life and the divine.

Each of these components contributes to the overall symbolism and beauty of the ofrenda, creating a sacred and vibrant space that exemplifies the essence of the Day of the Dead celebration—remembrance, connection, and the joyful embrace of life and death.

How to create a traditional altar

Creating a traditional Day of the Dead altar, or "ofrenda," is a heartfelt and symbolic process that involves careful consideration of the key components and their placement. Here's a step-by-step guide on how to create a traditional ofrenda:

1. Choose a Location:

Select a suitable location for your ofrenda. It can be set up in your home, in a community space, or even at a gravesite in a cemetery.

2. Prepare the Surface:

Place a table or a surface of your choice to serve as the base for your ofrenda. The table can be covered with a clean tablecloth in a bright color, such as white, to symbolize purity.

3. Create Levels:

Traditional ofrendas have multiple levels or tiers. You can use boxes, bricks, or other objects to create these levels. Each level represents a different realm: heaven, earth, and the underworld.

4. Marigold Flowers (Cempasúchil):

Arrange marigold flowers in intricate patterns or paths leading to the ofrenda. The bright colors and scent are believed to guide the spirits.

5. Candles (Veladoras):

Place candles on the ofrenda. These represent light, hope, and guidance for the spirits. You can use traditional votive candles or even LED candles for safety.

6. Incense (Copal):

Burn copal incense and let the fragrant smoke rise. It purifies the space and serves as a pathway for prayers to reach the spirits.

7. Papel Picado (Cut Paper Decorations):

Hang papel picado above the ofrenda to symbolize the fragility and beauty of life. You can purchase these decorations or make your own.

8. Calaveras (Sugar Skulls):

Include sugar skulls, either store-bought or homemade, on the ofrenda. You can personalize them with the names of your deceased loved ones.

9. Favorite Foods and Beverages:

Prepare the favorite foods and beverages of the deceased. These offerings are meant to nourish the spirits during their visit. Place these on the ofrenda along with plates, cups, and utensils.

10. Water:

Place a container of water on the ofrenda to quench the thirst of the spirits. You can also add a washbasin and soap for the spirits to cleanse themselves.

11. Salt:

Add a dish of salt on the ofrenda to purify the souls of the deceased. This symbolizes purification and preservation.

12. Photographs and Mementos:

Include framed photographs and personal mementos of the deceased on the ofrenda. This helps keep their memory alive and creates a visual connection.

13. Crosses and Religious Icons:

If you choose to incorporate religious symbols, place crosses and religious icons on the ofrenda to represent the spiritual journey of the deceased.

14. Personal Messages:

You can write personal messages or letters to your loved ones and place them on the ofrenda. These messages can express your feelings and memories.

15. Food and Drinks for Visitors:

Offer food and drinks for any living visitors or guests who come to pay their respects.

16. Offer Prayers and Remembrance:

Spend time in reflection, offering prayers, and sharing stories and memories of the deceased with family and friends who visit the ofrenda.

17. Light the Candles:

Light the candles on the ofrenda to create a warm and inviting atmosphere. The candles represent the guiding light for the spirits.

18. Visit and Share:

Encourage friends and family to visit the ofrenda, share stories, and partake in the foods and drinks you've prepared.

Creating a traditional ofrenda is a deeply personal and meaningful experience. It allows you to honor and remember your loved ones, and it symbolizes the enduring connection between the living and the departed. The act of creating and sharing an ofrenda is a beautiful and culturally rich way to celebrate the Day of the Dead.

Personalized altars and their importance

Personalized altars, or "ofrendas," are a significant and poignant aspect of the Day of the Dead celebration. They play a crucial role in connecting individuals and families to their deceased loved ones and in keeping their memories alive. Here's why personalized altars are important in this cultural tradition:

1. Honoring and Remembering Loved Ones:

Personalized altars provide a dedicated space for families to honor and remember their deceased relatives and friends. This act of remembrance is a way to pay tribute to the lives and legacies of those who have passed away.

2. Creating a Personal Connection:

By customizing the ofrenda with photographs, mementos, and favorite items of the deceased, individuals create a personal and emotional connection to their loved ones. It allows them to feel the presence of the departed and fosters a sense of continuity.

3. Emotional Healing:

The process of creating a personalized altar can be emotionally healing. It offers individuals an opportunity to grieve, reflect, and share stories about their loved ones. This cathartic experience can help with the grieving process.

4. Sharing Stories and Memories:

Personalized altars become spaces for storytelling and sharing anecdotes about the deceased. These stories serve to keep the memory of loved ones alive and ensure that their life experiences are passed down through generations.

5. Strengthening Family and Community Bonds:

The act of coming together to create and visit personalized altars fosters a sense of community and strengthens family bonds. It's a time when family and friends gather to honor their ancestors, share their experiences, and support one another in grief.

6. Cultural Identity and Heritage:

Personalized altars are a powerful expression of cultural identity and heritage. They showcase the unique customs and traditions of different families and communities, highlighting the rich tapestry of Mexican culture.

7. Bridging the Gap Between Worlds:

The ofrenda is believed to create a spiritual bridge between the living and the deceased. Personalized altars are a way for families to communicate with their departed loved ones, to express their love and gratitude, and to continue the relationship in a spiritual sense.

8. Embracing the Joy of Life:

The act of personalizing an altar is a celebration of life and a reminder that death is not to be feared. It emphasizes the joy of existence and the importance of cherishing every moment with loved ones.

9. Creative Expression:

Creating a personalized altar is an opportunity for artistic and creative expression. Families can showcase their craftsmanship by designing and decorating the ofrenda in a way that reflects their unique style.

In essence, personalized altars are a way to bring the past into the present, to celebrate life and death simultaneously, and to connect with the spiritual world. These altars are a tangible representation of the enduring bond between the living and the departed, ensuring that the memories of loved ones are cherished and preserved for generations to come.

Chapter Five: Traditional Foods and Drinks

Traditional foods and drinks play a central role in the Day of the Dead celebration, as they are offerings for the deceased and are also shared among the living as part of the festivities. These traditional items are rich in symbolism and flavor. Here are some of the most common traditional foods and drinks associated with the Day of the Dead:

1. Pan de Muerto (Bread of the Dead):

Description:

Pan de Muerto is a round or oval sweet bread with a slightly crusty outer layer and bone-shaped decorations on top, often made from sugar or dough.

Significance:

This bread symbolizes the circle of life and death, with the round shape representing the cyclical nature of existence. The bone shapes represent the deceased.

2. Mole:

Description:

Mole is a rich and complex sauce made from a mixture of ingredients, including chili peppers, chocolate, spices, and sometimes nuts or seeds. There are various types of mole, each with its unique flavor.

Significance:

Mole is a festive and flavorful dish served during the Day of the Dead to represent the celebration of life and the diversity of Mexican cuisine.

3. Tamales:

Description:

Tamales are a traditional Mexican dish made from masa (corn dough) filled with a variety of ingredients, such as meats, cheese, vegetables, and sauces. They are wrapped in corn husks and steamed.

Significance:

Tamales are a symbol of unity and the connections between people, as they are often made as a collaborative effort among family and friends.

4. Atole:

Description:

Atole is a warm, thick, and creamy beverage made from masa (corn dough), water or milk, and sweeteners like sugar, cinnamon, and vanilla.

Significance:

Atole is served as a comforting and nourishing drink during the Day of the Dead, providing warmth and sustenance for the spirits and the living.

5. Chocolate and Cocoa:

Description:

Chocolate is often used to make hot chocolate or champurrado (a thicker chocolate drink) during the celebration. Cocoa is a key ingredient in mole.

Significance:

Chocolate and cocoa symbolize the sweetness and richness of life, and they are often enjoyed during the festivities.

6. Favorite Foods of the Deceased:

Description:

On the ofrenda, families place the favorite foods and beverages of their deceased loved ones. These offerings can vary widely depending on personal preferences.

Significance:

Including the favorite foods of the deceased is a way to nourish their spirits during their visit and to show love and respect for their memory.

7. Agua de Jamaica (Hibiscus Tea) and Other Beverages:

Description:

Agua de Jamaica is a traditional Mexican beverage made from dried hibiscus flowers, water, and sugar. Other traditional drinks might include tequila, beer, or favorite soft drinks of the deceased.

Significance:

These beverages are served to quench the thirst of the spirits and are also enjoyed by the living during the celebration.

These traditional foods and drinks not only serve as offerings to the deceased but also enhance the sensory and cultural experience of the Day of the Dead. They reflect the vibrancy and diversity of Mexican cuisine and symbolize the connection between the living and the departed, as well as the celebration of life itself.

Traditional Day of the Dead dishes

Traditional Day of the Dead dishes vary by region and family traditions, but there are some iconic foods that are commonly associated with this celebration. Here are several traditional Day of the Dead dishes:

- **Mole:**

Mole is a rich and complex sauce made from chili peppers, chocolate, spices, and often includes ingredients like nuts, seeds, and fruit. It is typically served over chicken or turkey.

- **Pan de Muerto (Bread of the Dead):**

Pan de Muerto is a sweet, round bread with a slightly crusty outer layer and bone-shaped decorations on top, often made from sugar or dough. It's one of the most recognizable Day of the Dead foods.

- **Tamales:**

Tamales are made from masa (corn dough) and filled with a variety of ingredients such as meats, cheese, vegetables, or chiles. They are wrapped in corn husks and steamed.

- **Atole:**

Atole is a warm, thick, and creamy beverage made from masa, water or milk, and sweeteners like sugar, cinnamon, and vanilla. It's a comforting drink commonly enjoyed during the celebration.

- **Calabaza en Tacha (Candied Pumpkin):**

Calabaza en Tacha is made by simmering pumpkin in a syrup made from piloncillo (unrefined sugar) and flavored with cinnamon and other spices. It's a sweet treat often served during the festivities.

- **Candied Fruits and Sugar Skulls:**

Various fruits are candied and offered as sweet treats on the ofrenda. Sugar skulls, or calaveras de azúcar, are intricately decorated skull-shaped candies that are both decorative and edible.

- **Tortillas:**

Simple corn tortillas are often part of the Day of the Dead meal, serving as a staple in Mexican cuisine.

- **Tacos and Sopes:**

Some families include tacos or sopes (thicker, smaller tortillas with raised edges) as part of their Day of the Dead feast, filled with various ingredients like beans, meats, and vegetables.

- **Día de los Muertos Salad:**

This salad is made with jicama, oranges, and beets, creating a colorful and refreshing dish that represents the marigold flowers often used in the ofrendas.

- **Chocolate and Cocoa:**

Chocolate is used to make hot chocolate or champurrado, a thicker chocolate drink. Cocoa is also a key ingredient in mole.

- **Squash and Chiles:**

Various dishes may feature squash, often served as part of the mole, and chiles, which are integral to many Mexican recipes.

- **Favorite Foods of the Deceased:**

Families include the favorite foods and beverages of their deceased loved ones on the ofrenda, so these offerings can vary widely depending on personal preferences.

These traditional Day of the Dead dishes are a delightful combination of flavors and aromas that pay homage to the spirits of the departed. They serve as offerings to the deceased and are enjoyed by the living during the celebration, emphasizing the importance of sharing food and honoring the memory of loved ones.

Role of sugar skulls and pan de muerto

Sugar skulls (calaveras de azúcar) and Pan de Muerto are two iconic elements of the Day of the Dead celebration, and they play important roles in both the symbolism and traditions of this holiday.

Sugar Skulls (Calaveras de Azúcar):

- ## Symbol of Celebration:

Sugar skulls are whimsical and colorful representations of human skulls made from sugar, icing, and other confectionery decorations. They are not meant to be macabre; rather, they symbolize the celebration of life, the cycle of life and death, and the belief that death is a natural part of existence.

- ## Personalization:

Sugar skulls are often personalized with the names of deceased loved ones. By writing the names of the departed on the skulls, families pay tribute to those who have passed away and ensure that their memory lives on.

- **Decoration:**

Sugar skulls are used to decorate the ofrenda (altar) and are sometimes given as gifts to children or visitors during the Day of the Dead celebration. They can be beautifully crafted and intricately designed, showcasing the artistry and craftsmanship of the holiday.

- **Spiritual Offering:**

Sugar skulls serve as a form of offering to the spirits of the deceased. They are placed on the ofrenda to nourish and delight the souls of loved ones who have returned for a visit.

Pan de Muerto (Bread of the Dead):

- ### Circular Shape:

Pan de Muerto is a sweet, round bread with a slightly crusty outer layer and bone-shaped decorations on top. The circular shape of the bread represents the cyclical nature of life and death. It is symbolic of the never-ending cycle and the idea that death is not the end but a continuation of the journey.

- ### Sharing and Communion:

Families prepare Pan de Muerto as an offering for the deceased, placing it on the ofrenda to honor their memory. It is also a central element of the feast shared by the living, who gather to enjoy this delicious bread along with other traditional foods.

- ### Unity and Tradition:

Making Pan de Muerto is often a collaborative effort involving family members. This tradition of baking the bread together fosters unity, shared memories, and the passing down of cultural practices from one generation to the next.

- **Symbol of Death:**

The bone-shaped decorations on top of the bread are reminiscent of the deceased and are meant to be a representation of the bones of those who have passed. While this might seem somber, it is a way of acknowledging the presence of the spirits and offering them sustenance.

In summary, sugar skulls and Pan de Muerto are key elements of the Day of the Dead celebration. Sugar skulls represent the joy of life and personal remembrance, while Pan de Muerto symbolizes the cycle of life and death, unity within families, and the sharing of traditions. Both items are central to the expression of love and respect for the deceased and the celebration of life during this meaningful Mexican holiday.

Recipes and preparation methods

Certainly! Here are recipes and preparation methods for two traditional Day of the Dead dishes: Pan de Muerto (Bread of the Dead) and Atole. These recipes are adapted for home cooking and can be enjoyed as part of your Day of the Dead celebration.

Pan de Muerto (Bread of the Dead)

Ingredients:

- 4 cups all-purpose flour
- 1/2 cup sugar
- 1 packet (2 1/4 tsp) active dry yeast
- 1/2 cup whole milk
- 1/2 cup unsalted butter
- 4 large eggs
- 1/2 tsp salt
- 1/2 tsp anise extract (or orange blossom water)
- Zest of 1 orange
- 1 egg, beaten (for egg wash)
- Sugar for dusting

Instructions:

- In a small saucepan, heat the milk and butter over low heat until the butter is melted. Remove from heat and allow it to cool slightly.
- In a large mixing bowl, combine 2 cups of flour, sugar, yeast, and salt.
- Add the warm milk and butter mixture to the dry ingredients and mix well. Add the anise extract, orange zest, and 4 eggs. Stir until the dough starts to come together.
- Gradually add the remaining 2 cups of flour, one at a time, until a soft and slightly sticky dough forms.
- Turn the dough out onto a lightly floured surface and knead for about 8-10 minutes, or until it becomes smooth and elastic.
- Place the dough in a greased bowl, cover it with a clean kitchen towel, and let it rise in a warm, draft-free place for about 1-2 hours, or until it has doubled in size.

- Preheat your oven to 350°F (180°C).
- Divide the dough into portions to form the shape of the Pan de Muerto. Roll a large ball for the main part of the bread and smaller balls for the bones and decorations. Place the smaller dough pieces on top of the larger one, forming a cross shape.
- Brush the bread with the beaten egg and bake for 20-25 minutes, or until it's golden brown.
- While the bread is still warm, dust it with sugar for a sweet finish.

Atole

Ingredients:

- 1 cup masa harina (corn flour)
- 4 cups whole milk (or water)
- 1/2 cup sugar (adjust to taste)
- 1 tsp ground cinnamon
- 1 tsp vanilla extract
- A pinch of salt

Instructions:

1. In a bowl, mix the masa harina with 1 cup of milk (or water) until it forms a smooth paste.
2. In a large saucepan, combine the remaining 3 cups of milk, sugar, cinnamon, vanilla extract, and a pinch of salt. Heat over medium heat until it's warm but not boiling.
3. Gradually whisk the masa harina mixture into the warm milk, stirring constantly to avoid lumps.
4. Continue to cook the mixture over medium heat, stirring constantly, until it thickens to your desired consistency. It should be smooth and creamy, similar to a thick porridge.
5. Taste and adjust the sweetness with more sugar if needed.
6. Serve the atole warm in mugs or cups.

These recipes for Pan de Muerto and Atole are a delightful way to partake in the traditions of the Day of the Dead celebration and enjoy the flavors of Mexican cuisine. Feel free to personalize the recipes to your taste and enjoy them with your loved ones.

Chapter Six: Art and Craft

Art and craft play a significant role in the Day of the Dead celebration. They allow for creative expression and the crafting of intricate, meaningful items that are used in the ofrenda and throughout the festivities. Here are some key art and craft elements associated with the Day of the Dead:

1. Papel Picado (Cut Paper Decorations):

Papel picado is the art of cutting intricate designs into colorful tissue paper. These designs often feature skulls, flowers, and other symbols. Papel picado is used to decorate ofrendas and create an atmosphere of celebration.

2. Sugar Skulls (Calaveras de Azúcar):

Sugar skulls are handmade candies, often intricately decorated with bright colors and patterns. Crafting sugar skulls is a traditional art form that involves molding sugar into skull shapes, then adding details with icing and other edible decorations.

3. Skull Masks and Face Painting:

People often wear skull masks or paint their faces like skulls during Day of the Dead parades and celebrations. Creating or decorating these masks is a creative endeavor that allows individuals to participate in the cultural expression.

4. Marigold Flower Garlands:

Marigold flowers (cempasúchil) are a key symbol of the Day of the Dead. Crafting garlands and floral arrangements from marigolds is a way to honor the spirits and decorate ofrendas.

5. Ceramic and Clay Figures:

Artisans create ceramic and clay figurines that depict calacas (skeletons) engaged in various activities, such as musicians, dancers, or even couples in love. These figures are often used in ofrendas and as decorations.

6. Alebrijes:

Alebrijes are brightly colored Mexican folk art sculptures of fantastical creatures. They are often used in Day of the Dead celebrations, showcasing the creativity and artistry of Mexican artisans.

7. Altar Decorations:

Crafting decorations for the ofrenda is a deeply personal and artistic process. Families and individuals create custom items, including miniature items, candles, crosses, and religious icons.

8. Skull-Shaped Candles:

Artisanal candles in the shape of skulls are made for the Day of the Dead. These candles are often hand-painted with vibrant colors and designs.

9. Papier-Mâché Calacas:

Papier-mâché calacas (skeletons) are crafted and painted to represent various characters and activities. They are used in parades and are often part of ofrenda displays.

10. Personalized Altar Decor:

Crafting and personalizing the items on the ofrenda, such as sugar skulls with the names of the deceased, framed photographs, and other mementos, is a form of artistic expression that adds a deeply personal touch to the altar.

Art and craft in the Day of the Dead celebration not only beautify the event but also help convey the cultural and emotional significance of this holiday. They allow individuals and communities to express their creativity and love for their departed loved ones in a visual and tangible way, making the celebration even more meaningful.

Role of artistic expression in the ritual

Artistic expression plays a vital role in the Day of the Dead ritual, enriching the celebration in several ways:

1. Honoring the Deceased:

Artistic creations, such as sugar skulls, papel picado, and altars, serve as a form of tribute and remembrance for the deceased. They provide a visual and sensory way to honor the lives and memories of loved ones.

2. Symbolism and Meaning:

Artistic elements are rich in symbolism. They convey the messages of life, death, and rebirth, as well as the idea that death is a natural part of the human experience. For example, sugar skulls symbolize the celebration of life amidst mortality.

3. Bridging Worlds:

Artistic expressions are used to create a bridge between the living and the deceased.

The ofrenda, with its artistic decorations, serves as a spiritual meeting point where the realms of the living and the dead intersect.

4. Personalization:

Personalized art and craft items allow individuals and families to infuse their own emotions, memories, and creativity into the ritual. They enable a deeply personal connection to the celebration.

5. Creativity and Culture:

The creation of art and craft items for the Day of the Dead allows for the expression of cultural heritage and traditions. It showcases the artistic skills and talents of artisans and individuals within the community.

6. Shared Experience:

Artistic expression, such as face painting and mask making, is often a shared and communal experience. It brings people together to partake in the rituals, fostering a sense of togetherness and unity.

7. Visual Feast:

The colorful and vibrant artistic elements create a visually stimulating environment that draws people into the celebration. The ofrenda and the parade processions become a feast for the eyes, making the Day of the Dead a truly immersive experience.

8. Preservation of Traditions:

The creation of traditional art and craft items, such as papier-mâché calacas and alebrijes, helps preserve and pass down cultural traditions from one generation to the next.

9. Emotional Healing:

The act of creating and participating in artistic expressions can be emotionally healing. It allows people to process grief, share stories, and find comfort in the creative process.

10. Celebration of Life:

Artistic expression embodies the celebration of life amidst the awareness of death. It emphasizes that life is meant to be lived joyfully and that the deceased should be remembered with love and happiness.

In essence, artistic expression in the Day of the Dead ritual is a way to make the intangible tangible, to convey complex emotions and beliefs through visual and sensory means. It connects people to their cultural roots, their ancestors, and their own emotions, making the celebration a profound and beautiful experience.

Creating and decorating sugar skulls

Creating and decorating sugar skulls is a traditional and artistic part of the Day of the Dead celebration. These colorful and ornate skulls are both a form of art and a way to honor and remember the deceased. Here's a step-by-step guide on how to create and decorate sugar skulls:

Materials You'll Need:

- Granulated sugar (about 4 cups)
- Meringue powder (about 2 tablespoons)
- Water (about 2-3 tablespoons)
- Skull molds (available in various sizes and shapes)
- Royal icing (various colors)
- Food coloring (gel-based for vibrant colors)
- Edible decorations (such as sequins, mini flowers, edible glitter)
- Piping bags and tips (for decorating)

Creating Sugar Skulls:

Prepare the Sugar Mixture:

In a large mixing bowl, combine the granulated sugar and meringue powder.

Add Water:

Gradually add water, a little at a time, and mix until the sugar mixture holds its shape when squeezed. You want it to have the consistency of damp sand.

Pack the Skull Molds:

Fill the sugar skull molds with the sugar mixture, pressing it down firmly to ensure it holds its shape. Overfill the molds, and then use a flat edge to level the sugar on top.

Compact the Mixture:

Use a wooden spoon or your fingers to compact the sugar mixture further. The skulls need to be tightly packed to hold together.

Unmold the Skulls:

Gently tap the molds to release the sugar skulls onto a tray or baking sheet. Be patient and delicate to avoid damaging the skulls.

Dry the Skulls:

Allow the sugar skulls to air dry for at least 8-12 hours or overnight. They need to harden and become solid.

Decorating Sugar Skulls:

Prepare Royal Icing:

Make royal icing by mixing powdered sugar with a small amount of water until you achieve a thick but spreadable consistency. Divide the icing into small bowls and add food coloring to create vibrant colors.

Decorate with Royal Icing:

Use the colored royal icing to create designs, patterns, and features on the sugar skulls. You can paint the entire skull with a base color, add intricate designs, and create eyes, noses, and mouths. Be creative and use a variety of colors and patterns.

Add Edible Decorations:

While the icing is still wet, you can add edible decorations like sequins, mini flowers, or edible glitter to enhance the beauty of the sugar skulls.

Allow to Dry:

Let the decorated sugar skulls dry for a few hours or until the icing hardens. The drying time can vary depending on the thickness of the icing.

Display and Share:

Once the sugar skulls are completely dry, they are ready to be displayed on the ofrenda or given as gifts to friends and family. They serve as a colorful and edible tribute to the deceased.

Creating and decorating sugar skulls is a joyful and artistic process that allows you to infuse your own creativity and personal touch into the Day of the Dead celebration. It's a meaningful way to honor your loved ones and engage in the rich traditions of this cultural celebration.

Papel picado and other traditional crafts

Papel picado and other traditional crafts are integral to the Day of the Dead celebration, as they add a decorative and symbolic element to the rituals and festivities. Here's an overview of papel picado and other traditional crafts associated with this holiday:

1. Papel Picado (Cut Paper Decorations):

- *Description:*

Papel picado involves the intricate cutting of colorful tissue paper into various designs, including skulls, flowers, and geometric patterns. The cut paper is hung on strings to create banners or decorations.

- *Significance:*

Papel picado represents the fragility and beauty of life. The designs, often featuring skeletons and other Day of the Dead symbols, are meant to celebrate and remember the deceased.

2. Sugar Skulls (Calaveras de Azúcar):

- *Description:*

Sugar skulls are handcrafted candies made from sugar, molded into skull shapes, and elaborately decorated with icing, sequins, and colorful designs.

- *Significance:*

Sugar skulls are used to honor and remember the departed. They symbolize the sweetness of life and the idea that death is just a part of the cycle.

3. Ceramic and Clay Figurines:

- *Description:*

Artisans create ceramic and clay figurines, often depicting calacas (skeletons), in various scenes and activities. These figurines come in all sizes and are sometimes used to represent individuals or activities associated with the deceased.

- *Significance:*

These figurines are both artistic and symbolic. They showcase the creativity of Mexican artisans and contribute to the festive atmosphere.

4. Alebrijes:

- *Description:*

Alebrijes are brightly colored Mexican folk art sculptures of fantastical creatures. They are often hand-carved from wood and painted in intricate patterns and designs.

- *Significance:*

While alebrijes are not exclusive to the Day of the Dead, they are sometimes incorporated into the celebration for their vibrant and imaginative qualities. They represent the spirit of creativity and the fantastical elements of Mexican art.

5. Papier-Mâché Calacas:

- *Description:*

Papier-mâché calacas (skeletons) are crafted and painted to represent various characters and activities, from musicians to calavera brides and grooms.

- *Significance:*

These figures are used in parades and as part of ofrenda displays to add a touch of whimsy and culture to the celebration.

6. Candle Decorations:

- *Description:*

Handcrafted candles, often in the shape of skulls or crosses, are used to illuminate the ofrenda and other spaces during the celebration.

- *Significance:*

These candles represent the guiding light for the spirits, offering a warm and inviting atmosphere during the Day of the Dead.

7. Floral Arrangements:

- *Description:*

Marigold flowers (cempasúchil) are used to create floral arrangements, wreaths, and garlands to decorate the ofrenda and other spaces.

- *Significance:*

Marigolds are believed to guide the spirits with their vibrant colors and scent. They are also symbolic of the sun and life.

8. Crosses and Religious Icons:

- *Description:*

Crosses, religious icons, and other religious crafts are sometimes included in the ofrenda to represent the spiritual journey of the deceased.

- *Significance:*

These items reflect the spiritual and religious aspects of the celebration, acknowledging the connection between life and the afterlife.

These traditional crafts contribute to the visual richness and cultural significance of the Day of the Dead celebration. They are a testament to the creativity and artistry of the Mexican people and serve as tangible expressions of love and remembrance for the deceased.

Music and dance are integral components of the Day of the Dead celebration, adding to the festive and joyful atmosphere. They play a crucial role in honoring the deceased and connecting the living with the spiritual world. Here are some key elements of music and dance in the Day of the Dead:

1. Calaveras (Skull) Songs:

- *Description:*

Calaveras are humorous or satirical poems or songs that mock death and the deceased in a lighthearted manner. They often depict the deceased as having a lively personality even in death.

- *Significance:*

Calaveras are a way to embrace the concept of death with humor and irreverence. They are a form of social commentary that celebrates life and mocks the fear of death.

2. Traditional Mexican Music:

- *Description:*

Various styles of traditional Mexican music, including mariachi, ranchera, and bolero, are commonly heard during the Day of the Dead celebration. These musical genres use instruments such as trumpets, guitars, and violins.

- *Significance:*

Traditional Mexican music adds a festive and cultural dimension to the celebration. Mariachi bands are often part of parades and processions.

3. Danza de los Viejitos (Dance of the Old Men):

- *Description:*

Danza de los Viejitos is a traditional dance performed by men dressed as elderly individuals. They wear masks and colorful clothing and engage in humorous and playful movements.

- *Significance:*

This dance serves to emphasize the humor and joy of life and death. It's a way to acknowledge the cycle of life and the wisdom of the elderly.

4. La Calavera Catrina Dance:

- *Description:*

La Calavera Catrina is an iconic image of a well-dressed skeleton lady. Dancers sometimes portray La Catrina and engage in elegant and stylized dances.

- *Significance:*

The dance of La Calavera Catrina celebrates the blending of life and death, beauty and mortality, and is a reminder that death does not discriminate.

5. Aztec Dances:

- *Description:*

Some Day of the Dead celebrations incorporate traditional Aztec dances. These dances often feature vibrant and elaborate costumes and are performed to the beat of ancient drums.

- *Significance:*

Aztec dances connect the Day of the Dead celebration to Mexico's indigenous history and pay homage to the cultural diversity within the country.

6. Traditional Folk Dances:

- *Description:*

Various traditional folk dances, such as the Jarabe Tapatío (Mexican Hat Dance) and La Negra, are performed during the celebration.

- *Significance:*

These dances showcase the regional diversity of Mexico's culture and are a way to honor the traditions of specific communities.

7. Processions and Parades:

- *Description:*

Parades and processions are a common feature of Day of the Dead celebrations, often accompanied by music, dance, and colorful costumes.

- *Significance:*

These processions bring communities together to celebrate and honor the deceased. They create a sense of unity and shared purpose.

8. Music and Dance in Cemeteries:

- *Description:*

In many regions, families visit cemeteries to be with their loved ones. They bring musicians, and people often dance and sing in the presence of the deceased.

- *Significance:*

This practice is a way to communicate with the spirits, to celebrate their memory, and to feel a connection to the afterlife.

Music and dance infuse the Day of the Dead celebration with life, energy, and cultural expression. They are a way to honor the deceased, find joy in the face of death, and create a bridge between the living and the spiritual world, making the holiday a truly unique and meaningful event.

Traditional Day of the Dead music

Traditional Day of the Dead music encompasses a variety of genres and styles, reflecting the rich musical heritage of Mexico. Here are some traditional types of music commonly associated with the Day of the Dead celebration:

1. Mariachi Music:

Mariachi is perhaps the most iconic and well-known style of Mexican music. Mariachi bands, often dressed in charro outfits, play a range of instruments, including trumpets, violins, and guitars. They perform lively and emotional ranchera songs that can capture the essence of the Day of the Dead.

2. Ranchera Music:

Ranchera is a genre of traditional Mexican music that often tells stories of love, loss, and the Mexican way of life. These songs frequently use guitars, trumpets, and violins and are a staple of Day of the Dead celebrations.

3. Bolero Music:

Bolero is a romantic genre characterized by its slow tempo and heartfelt lyrics. While it may not seem like an obvious choice for the festive Day of the Dead, boleros can be sung to remember and honor loved ones who have passed away.

4. Corridos:

Corridos are narrative ballads that tell stories of people's lives, including historical events and legendary figures. They can be used to recount the lives and adventures of the deceased.

5. Son Jarocho:

Originating from the Veracruz region, Son Jarocho is a folk style of music that often features the use of the harp, jarana (a small guitar-like instrument), and requinto (a small guitar). This lively music and dance style is sometimes incorporated into Day of the Dead celebrations.

6. Pre-Hispanic Music:

Some Day of the Dead celebrations include traditional pre-Hispanic music, which involves the use of indigenous instruments like drums, flutes, and rattles. This music connects the celebration to Mexico's indigenous roots.

7. Traditional Folk Songs:

In various regions of Mexico, traditional folk songs and dances are performed during the Day of the Dead. These songs may have regional variations and showcase the diversity of Mexican culture.

8. Cumbia and Salsa:

In some regions, upbeat Latin dance music like cumbia and salsa is integrated into the Day of the Dead celebrations, providing an opportunity for dancing and lively festivities.

9. Aztec and Indigenous Music:

Indigenous music, such as Aztec drumming and flute playing, connects the celebration to Mexico's ancient traditions and rituals.

10. Contemporary Music:

While traditional music plays a significant role in the Day of the Dead, contemporary songs and musical styles are also part of their celebrations, reflecting the evolving nature of the holiday.

The choice of music during Day of the Dead celebrations can vary depending on the region and the personal preferences of the participants. It is common to hear a mix of traditional and contemporary music, all contributing to the vibrant and lively atmosphere of this cultural holiday.

Regional dance styles and their meanings

Regional dance styles are an integral part of Day of the Dead celebrations in Mexico. Each region has its unique dances, often accompanied by distinct costumes, music, and symbolism. These dances serve to honor the deceased and convey the cultural diversity of Mexico. Here are some regional dance styles and their meanings:

1. Danza de los Viejitos (Dance of the Old Men):

Region: Michoacán

Description:

Dancers, dressed as elderly individuals, wear masks and colorful clothing. The dance involves playful and humorous movements.

Meaning:

This dance celebrates the wisdom and experiences of the elderly, emphasizing the continuity of life and death.

2. La Calavera Catrina Dance:

Region: Mexico City and Central Mexico

Description:

Dancers, sometimes portraying La Calavera Catrina, engage in elegant and stylized movements, often wearing elaborate costumes and makeup.

Meaning:

This dance symbolizes the blending of life and death, beauty and mortality. It conveys the idea that death is an intrinsic part of life.

3. Danza de los Tecuanes (Tecuanes Dance):

Region: Guerrero

Description:

Dancers perform the Tecuanes Dance in which they take on the roles of jaguars and hunters. It's a lively and dynamic dance.

Meaning:

The dance reenacts the struggle between jaguars and hunters, symbolizing the ongoing cycle of life and death in nature.

4. Danza de los Diablos (Dance of the Devils):

Region: Oaxaca

Description:

Dancers don devil costumes, complete with masks and suits adorned with bells, and perform intricate choreography.

Meaning:

The dance serves to confront and mock death. It reflects the belief that, even in death, one can find humor and defiance.

5. Danza de la Pluma (Feather Dance):

Region: Oaxaca

Description:

Dancers wear traditional feathered costumes and perform a symbolic narrative, often reenacting historic or mythological stories.

Meaning:

The Danza de la Pluma is a complex narrative dance that may not be specific to the Day of the Dead, but it is an important tradition in Oaxaca that can be incorporated into the celebrations.

6. Xantolo (Day of the Dead Festival):

Region: Hidalgo and San Luis Potosí

Description:

Xantolo is a regional festival that includes various traditional dances, such as the Danza del Xantolo, performed by indigenous Huastec communities.

Meaning:

These dances are part of the Xantolo festival, celebrating the deceased and the Huastec culture. They reflect a deep connection to ancestral traditions.

7. Danza de la Conquista (Conquest Dance):

Region: Chiapas

Description:

Dancers, dressed as indigenous people and Spanish conquistadors, perform a historical narrative dance.

Meaning:

This dance reenacts the encounter between indigenous cultures and the Spanish conquistadors, reflecting the intersection of cultures and history.

These regional dance styles offer a glimpse into the diverse cultural tapestry of Mexico. They are performed with pride and reverence during the Day of the Dead celebration, emphasizing the significance of the holiday as a time to remember, honor, and celebrate the lives of those who have passed away.

Contemporary adaptations and influences

Contemporary adaptations and influences have shaped the way the Day of the Dead is celebrated in the modern era. While the core traditions and symbolism remain intact, various factors have contributed to the evolution of this cultural celebration. Here are some of the contemporary adaptations and influences on the Day of the Dead:

1. Global Awareness:

The Day of the Dead has gained global recognition and popularity. Many people outside of Mexico now celebrate and appreciate the holiday, leading to cross-cultural influences and adaptations.

2. Artistic Expression:

Contemporary artists have played a significant role in reimagining and expanding the artistic aspects of the celebration. From contemporary art exhibitions to multimedia installations, the artistic interpretations of the Day of the Dead have evolved.

3. Commercialization:

The holiday has seen commercial influences, with the sale of Day of the Dead-themed merchandise and products. This has led to a broader awareness of the celebration but also concerns about cultural appropriation.

4. Social Media and Pop Culture:

The prevalence of social media and pop culture has brought Day of the Dead into mainstream awareness. It's now a common theme in films, TV shows, and advertising campaigns.

5. Interfaith and Inter-Cultural Dialogue:

Interfaith and inter-cultural dialogues have shaped the way Day of the Dead is celebrated by individuals from diverse backgrounds. People of various religious and cultural backgrounds may incorporate elements of the celebration into their own practices.

6. Personalization and Creativity:

Many individuals and communities have personalized the Day of the Dead to reflect their own experiences and beliefs. They may incorporate new elements, themes, or artistic expressions into their celebrations.

7. Environmental Consciousness:

Some contemporary adaptations include a focus on environmental sustainability. Efforts are made to reduce waste and minimize the environmental impact of the celebration, such as using biodegradable materials for ofrendas and decorations.

8. Expanded Meaning and Inclusivity:

Some contemporary celebrations seek to broaden the Day of the Dead's meaning to encompass various aspects of remembrance, including commemorating social justice movements, honoring deceased pets, or addressing current global issues.

9. Diaspora Communities:

Mexican diaspora communities around the world have adapted the Day of the Dead to their local environments while retaining its core traditions. This has resulted in unique variations of the celebration in different countries.

10. Cultural Exchange:

International cultural exchange programs and festivals have contributed to a sharing of traditions. Mexican communities abroad often host Day of the Dead events to share their culture with others.

These contemporary adaptations and influences reflect the dynamic nature of culture and how traditions can evolve while retaining their core values. The Day of the

Dead continues to be a meaningful and vibrant celebration that bridges the past with the present and transcends cultural boundaries.

Chapter Eight: The Marigold Path (Cempasúchil)

The Marigold Path, known as "La Senda de Cempasúchil" in Spanish, is a symbolic element of the Day of the Dead celebration in Mexico. Cempasúchil is the native Nahuatl name for marigold flowers, which have deep cultural and spiritual significance in this holiday. Here's an explanation of the Marigold Path and its role in the Day of the Dead:

1. Significance of Marigolds:

Marigold flowers (cempasúchil) hold special importance in the Day of the Dead tradition. Their vibrant orange and yellow hues are believed to represent the sun, life, and resurrection. These flowers are thought to help guide the spirits of the deceased back to the world of the living.

2. Creating the Marigold Path:

Families and communities often create paths or elaborate floral arrangements made of marigold petals. These paths may lead from the cemetery's entrance to the gravesites or from the altar (ofrenda) to other areas of the celebration.

3. Symbolism:

The Marigold Path symbolizes a welcoming and guiding route for the spirits of the deceased. It is believed that the strong scent of marigolds helps lead the spirits back to the world of the living during the Day of the Dead.

4. Use in Ofrendas:

Marigold flowers are a common addition to ofrendas (altars) dedicated to the deceased. They are often placed alongside photographs, favorite foods, and mementos of the departed. The bright marigold petals are meant to attract the spirits with their vibrant color and fragrance.

5. Floral Archways:

In some regions, marigold petals are used to create beautiful archways or intricate designs, like marigold carpets. These archways can be found in cemeteries, homes, and public spaces, adding to the visual richness of the Day of the Dead.

6. Cultural Variations:

While the Marigold Path is a common feature in many Day of the Dead celebrations, its design and extent can vary from one region to another. Some communities may create more elaborate and extensive paths, while others may keep it simple.

7. Preservation Efforts:

In recent years, there has been an emphasis on using organic and biodegradable materials in the Marigold Path and other Day of the Dead decorations to minimize environmental impact.

The Marigold Path is a powerful and poignant element of the Day of the Dead, reflecting the belief that life and death are part of a continuous cycle. The fragrance and vibrant colors of marigolds are believed to bridge the gap between the living and the deceased, creating a visual and sensory tribute to those who have passed away.

The significance of marigolds in the celebration

Marigolds, known as "cempasúchil" in Nahuatl and "flor de muerto" or "flor de los difuntos" in Spanish, hold significant cultural and symbolic importance in the Day of the Dead celebration in Mexico. Their presence and use during this holiday convey several layers of meaning and tradition:

1. Representing the Sun and Life:

Marigold flowers are often vibrant orange or yellow, colors that symbolize the sun. In Mexican culture, the sun is associated with life, warmth, and energy. Marigolds, with their radiant hues, are believed to symbolize the light and vitality of the living world.

2. Attracting and Guiding Spirits:

It is believed that the spirits of the deceased are drawn to the scent and color of marigolds. The strong, sweet aroma is thought to help guide the souls back to the world of the living during the Day of the Dead. Marigolds are often used to create paths and decorations to guide the spirits to ofrendas (altars) and graves.

3. Blending Indigenous and Catholic Traditions:

The use of marigolds in the Day of the Dead blends indigenous Mexican traditions with Catholic beliefs. Indigenous cultures in Mexico held the marigold in high regard for its symbolic and medicinal properties. By incorporating marigolds into the Day of the Dead, a connection is made between pre-Hispanic beliefs and the Christian influence on Mexican culture.

4. Petals as Pathways:

Marigold petals are often used to create intricate designs and paths on the ground. These paths, known as the Marigold Path, lead the spirits to their ofrendas and graves. The concept of marigold paths underscores the idea of a safe and welcoming journey for the deceased.

5. Adding Fragrance and Beauty to Ofrendas:

Marigold flowers are commonly included in ofrendas. They are placed on altars along with other offerings like food, candles, and photos of the deceased. The marigolds contribute to the visual appeal and fragrance of the ofrenda, enhancing the experience for both the living and the spirits.

6. Bridging Life and Death:

The Day of the Dead is a celebration of life within the context of death. Marigolds symbolize this dual nature of the holiday by embodying the vibrancy of life and the recognition of mortality. They serve as a reminder that death is a natural part of the human experience.

7. Cultural Pride and Identity:

Marigolds are deeply rooted in Mexican culture and are a source of pride and identity. Their significance in the Day of the Dead highlights the connection between cultural heritage and the spiritual aspect of the celebration.

Marigolds, with their color, fragrance, and symbolism, are a unifying and culturally rich element in the Day of the Dead. They not only serve a practical purpose in guiding and honoring the spirits but also provide a powerful visual representation of the cycle of life and death, making them an integral part of this unique Mexican tradition.

How they are used to create paths and decorations

Marigolds are used to create paths and decorations in the Day of the Dead celebration in various ways. These floral arrangements play a vital role in guiding the spirits of the deceased and adding vibrant beauty to the festivities. Here's how marigolds are used to create paths and decorations:

1. Marigold Paths (La Senda de Cempasúchil):

Marigold paths are created on the ground, leading from the entrance of a cemetery to the gravesites or from the altar (ofrenda) to other areas of the celebration. The path often forms a colorful carpet of marigold petals.

2. Preparation:

To create a Marigold Path, people collect marigold flowers and carefully pluck the petals, leaving the stems behind. The petals are spread out in a continuous line to form the path.

3. Design and Patterns:

The petals can be arranged to create intricate patterns, symbols, or images along the path. Sometimes, designs may include the deceased's name, messages, or religious symbols.

4. Cemetery Decorations:

In cemeteries, marigold paths often extend from the entrance to specific gravesites. They create a visually stunning and symbolic route for the spirits to follow when they return to the world of the living.

5. Ofrenda Decorations:

Marigold petals are also used to decorate the ofrenda. They may be arranged in patterns, surrounding the offerings, photos, and mementos dedicated to the deceased. The bright petals add color and fragrance to the altar.

6. Archways and Floral Arrangements:

Marigold petals are used to create archways, garlands, and floral arrangements. These archways are often placed at entrances to cemeteries or around ofrendas. They may include marigolds and other flowers, such as chrysanthemums and roses.

7. Symbolic Elements:

Marigold paths and decorations may include other symbolic elements like candles, sugar skulls, and incense. These elements enhance the visual and sensory experience of the celebration.

8. Biodegradable Materials:

In recent years, there has been an emphasis on using organic and biodegradable materials for Marigold Paths and decorations to minimize the environmental impact of the celebration.

Marigold paths and decorations are not only visually stunning but also serve a deeply spiritual purpose. They are believed to help guide the spirits of the deceased back to the world of the living, providing a warm and inviting route for the souls to follow. Marigolds, with their vibrant colors and sweet fragrance, play a central role in creating a sensory-rich and meaningful atmosphere during the Day of the Dead celebration.

Marigolds in Mexican folklore

Marigolds, known as "cempasúchil" in Nahuatl and "flor de muerto" or "flor de los difuntos" in Spanish, have a rich and significant presence in Mexican folklore, culture, and tradition. They are revered for their symbolism and uses beyond just the Day of the Dead. Here are some aspects of marigolds in Mexican folklore:

1. Symbol of the Sun:

In Aztec mythology, marigolds were associated with the sun god, Huitzilopochtli. The bright and vibrant colors of marigolds were seen as symbolic of the sun's radiant energy. The marigold's essence was thought to bring light and vitality.

2. Spiritual and Medicinal Uses:

Indigenous cultures in Mexico held marigolds in high regard for their spiritual and medicinal properties. They were believed to have protective qualities and were used in traditional remedies to treat various ailments.

3. Celebratory Events:

Marigolds are often used in various celebrations and festivals in Mexico. They are incorporated into decorations for weddings, religious ceremonies, and other special occasions, symbolizing joy and celebration.

4. Pest Control:

Marigolds have natural pesticide properties due to their strong aroma and natural compounds. In Mexican folklore, they are planted in gardens to repel pests and protect other plants.

5. Religious Significance:

In Catholicism, marigolds are sometimes associated with the Virgin Mary and are used in religious processions and offerings.

The bright colors are seen as a symbol of the divine.

6. Altar Decorations:

Marigolds are a common feature on ofrendas (altars) not only during the Day of the Dead but also in various religious and cultural celebrations. They are placed as offerings to honor saints, religious figures, and deceased loved ones.

7. Protective Properties:

Marigolds are believed to have protective qualities against negative energies and evil spirits. They are sometimes used in rituals to cleanse and purify spaces.

8. Seasonal Festivals:

Marigolds play a significant role in various Mexican festivals and rituals throughout the year. They are especially prominent in the Day of the Dead, where they guide the spirits of the deceased with their bright colors and fragrance.

9. Art and Craft:

Marigold petals are used for creating intricate designs, artwork, and floral arrangements. They are also featured in traditional folk art, including papel picado and pottery.

10. Cultural Identity:

Marigolds are an essential part of Mexican cultural identity. They are a symbol of the connection between ancient indigenous beliefs and contemporary Mexican culture.

Marigolds are deeply interwoven with Mexican folklore and are celebrated not only for their visual and aromatic qualities but also for their cultural and spiritual significance. They embody the essence of life, death, and the enduring spirit of Mexican traditions.

Chapter Nine: Calaveras (Skeletons)

Calaveras, which are often depicted as skeletons or skulls, are iconic symbols of the Day of the Dead (Día de los Muertos) in Mexico. These representations of skeletal figures hold significant cultural and artistic value in the celebration and are used in various forms, including calavera makeup, costumes, and artwork. Here's an overview of calaveras in the context of the Day of the Dead:

1. La Catrina:

La Catrina is one of the most famous calaveras. She is depicted as an elegantly dressed skeleton with a wide-brimmed hat. La Catrina was created by the Mexican artist José Guadalupe Posada and later popularized by Diego Rivera's mural. She is a satirical representation of death and a reminder that death does not discriminate based on social class or wealth.

2. Artistic Expression:

Calaveras are a prominent theme in Day of the Dead artwork. They are often depicted in paintings, sculptures, and papier-mâché figures. These representations can vary from comical and whimsical to intricate and thought-provoking.

3. Calaveras in Literature:

Calaveras are featured in literary works, including calavera poems (calacas) that humorously portray the living as skeletons. These poems often mock people's habits, behaviors, and circumstances.

4. Calavera Makeup and Costumes:

During Day of the Dead celebrations, it's common for people to paint their faces as calaveras using intricate designs. They may wear costumes or accessories that represent skeletons, embracing the idea of death as a part of life.

5. Role in Ofrendas:

Calavera figurines, often dressed as musicians or engaged in daily activities, are sometimes placed on ofrendas (altars) to symbolize the continuation of life beyond death. These figurines are made from various materials, including clay and sugar.

6. Social and Political Commentary:

Calaveras are sometimes used as a form of social and political satire in Mexico. They can be employed to comment on current events, political figures, or societal issues.

7. Public Displays and Parades:

Calavera imagery is often featured in Day of the Dead parades and public displays. Large calavera puppets and floats are used to engage and entertain the crowds.

8. Symbol of the Cycle of Life and Death:

Calaveras are a reminder of the cyclical nature of life and death. They represent the idea that death is not an end but a continuation of the journey. They are a celebration of the connection between the living and the deceased.

9. Personal Connection:

Families often personalize calaveras to represent deceased loved ones. These customized calaveras may include the names and characteristics of the individuals they are honoring.

10. Cultural Identity:

Calaveras are a distinctive part of Mexican culture and identity. They are a symbol of the Mexican people's unique way of embracing and commemorating death.

Calaveras are a creative and symbolic expression of the Day of the Dead, adding depth and cultural richness to the celebration. They convey the message that death should not be feared but rather embraced as an integral part of life's journey.

History and symbolism of calaveras

The history and symbolism of calaveras, which are skeletal figures or skulls, are deeply rooted in Mexican culture and have evolved over time. Here's an exploration of the history and symbolism of calaveras:

Historical Origins:

Calaveras have their origins in ancient Mesoamerican cultures, where the concept of death and the afterlife played a central role in religious beliefs. The Aztecs, for instance, had a goddess of death called Mictecacihuatl. Skulls and skeletal imagery were common in their rituals and art.

José Guadalupe Posada:

The modern calavera imagery was popularized by the Mexican artist José Guadalupe Posada (1852-1913). Posada was known for his satirical illustrations, and he created numerous engravings featuring skeletal figures, often dressed in clothing or engaging in everyday activities. These calaveras were accompanied by humorous or critical verses.

La Catrina:

One of Posada's most famous calavera creations is "La Catrina." This elegant female skeleton, dressed in early 20th-century upper-class attire, has become an iconic representation of death. La Catrina is a satirical character that mocks those who pretend to be of higher social status, emphasizing the idea that death is the great equalizer.

Diego Rivera's Mural:

The Mexican muralist Diego Rivera featured La Catrina in his mural "Sueño de una Tarde Dominical en la Alameda Central" (Dream of a Sunday Afternoon in the Alameda Central), which was completed in 1947. In this mural, La Catrina is depicted alongside historical and political figures, underscoring the theme of the passage of time and the universality of death.

Day of the Dead (Día de los Muertos):

Calaveras are central to the Day of the Dead celebration in Mexico. During this holiday, people use calavera imagery in various forms, such as sugar skulls (calaveras de azúcar), calavera makeup, and calavera figurines. The use of calaveras during the Day of the Dead symbolizes the connection between the living and the deceased and serves as a way to honor and remember loved ones who have passed away.

Satirical Poetry:

Calaveras are featured in calavera poems, also known as "calacas." These satirical poems humorously depict people as skeletons and are a common form of expression during the Day of the Dead. They often playfully critique individuals' quirks, habits, and experiences.

Cycle of Life and Death:

Calaveras symbolize the cyclical nature of life and death. They are a reminder that death is not an end but a part of the ongoing journey. The bright and vibrant colors of calaveras emphasize the celebration of life and the acceptance of mortality.

Personalization and Remembrance:

Families often personalize calaveras to represent deceased loved ones. These customized calaveras may include the names and characteristics of the individuals they are honoring, making them a heartfelt tribute.

Calaveras, with their rich history and symbolism, are a testament to the Mexican perspective on death. They convey the idea that death should not be feared but embraced as an integral part of the human experience, celebrated with humor, reverence, and remembrance during the Day of the Dead and beyond.

Literary and artistic representations of calaveras

Calaveras, which are often depicted as skeletons or skulls, have inspired a wide range of literary and artistic representations in Mexican and broader cultural contexts. These representations are used to explore themes of mortality, the afterlife, and the connection between the living and the deceased. Here are some examples of literary and artistic representations of calaveras:

1. Calavera Poetry (Calacas):

Calavera poetry, also known as "calacas," is a traditional form of satire during the Day of the Dead. These humorous poems and verses often depict people as skeletons and mock their quirks and foibles. The most famous calavera poem is "La Calavera Catrina" by José Guadalupe Posada, which satirizes the Mexican elite.

2. Posada's Calavera Engravings:

José Guadalupe Posada, a Mexican artist, is renowned for his calavera engravings. These detailed and satirical illustrations feature skeletal figures dressed in various roles, from musicians and politicians to ordinary people. His work has had a profound influence on the popular perception of calaveras.

3. Diego Rivera's Mural:

Diego Rivera's mural "Sueño de una Tarde Dominical en la Alameda Central" prominently features La Catrina, a satirical representation of death, among other historical and political figures. Rivera's mural is a powerful example of the use of calavera imagery in Mexican art to convey social and political commentary.

4. Skull Art and Decorations:

Calavera imagery is commonly used in various forms of art and craft, including paintings, sculptures, papier-mâché figures, and jewelry. Skull-themed artwork is not limited to the Day of the Dead but is also embraced in contemporary art and pop culture.

5. Calavera Makeup and Costumes:

During the Day of the Dead, people paint their faces as calaveras using intricate designs. This calavera makeup is a form of artistic expression and participation in the celebration.

6. Day of the Dead Altars (Ofrendas):

Calavera figurines, often dressed in festive attire or engaged in various activities, are placed on ofrendas (altars) to honor the deceased. These figurines symbolize the continuity of life and death and add artistic elements to the ofrendas.

7. Public Displays and Parades:

Calavera imagery is featured in public displays and parades during the Day of the Dead. Large calavera puppets, floats, and art installations are used to engage and entertain the crowds, contributing to the festive and artistic atmosphere.

8. Literature and Novels:

Calaveras have been featured in Mexican literature and novels. They are often used as metaphors or symbols to explore themes of life, death, and the human condition.

9. Film and Animation:

Calaveras have appeared in animated films, particularly those inspired by the Day of the Dead. For example, the 2017 animated film "Coco" is known for its depiction of calaveras and their role in the afterlife.

10. Street Art and Graffiti:

Calavera imagery is also found in street art and graffiti, reflecting contemporary social and political commentary, as well as celebrating Mexican culture.

Calaveras, in their literary and artistic forms, serve as a vibrant and multifaceted expression of Mexican culture and the way in which death is embraced, celebrated, and used to explore various aspects of the human experience. They represent both the humorous and the profound aspects of the human condition.

Role of calaveras in Day of the Dead celebrations

Calaveras play a central and multifaceted role in the Day of the Dead (Día de los Muertos) celebrations in Mexico. These skeletal figures, often represented as skulls, are integral to the holiday's cultural, artistic, and spiritual aspects. Here are the key roles of calaveras in Day of the Dead celebrations:

1. Symbol of Death and the Afterlife:

Calaveras are a symbolic representation of death itself. They serve as a reminder of the impermanence of life and the belief that death is not an end but a continuation of the journey.

2. Honoring the Deceased:

Calaveras are used to honor and remember deceased loved ones. Families personalize calaveras, often inscribing the names of the departed on them. These customized calaveras may be displayed on ofrendas (altars) dedicated to the deceased.

3. Mocking and Satire:

Calaveras are used in calavera poems and literature to humorously satirize the living. These poems poke fun at people's quirks, habits, and behaviors, emphasizing the idea that death does not discriminate based on social class or status.

4. Artistic Expression:

Calaveras provide a creative outlet for artistic expression during the Day of the Dead. Artists and craftsmen create intricate calavera artwork, including sculptures, paintings, and papier-mâché figures.

5. Calavera Makeup and Costumes:

People, young and old, engage in calavera makeup and costumes during the celebrations. They paint their faces as skeletons, wear skeleton-themed clothing, and participate in parades and gatherings, adding a festive and artistic element to the holiday.

6. Public Displays and Parades:

Calavera imagery is prominently featured in public displays and parades. Large calavera puppets, floats, and art installations are used to engage the public and celebrate the Day of the Dead.

7. Connection to La Catrina:

La Catrina, an elegant female skeleton, is one of the most iconic calaveras and is closely associated with the Day of the Dead. She symbolizes the idea that death does not distinguish between social classes and that all are equal in death.

8. Cultural Identity:

Calaveras are a distinct and recognizable part of Mexican cultural identity. They reflect the Mexican people's unique way of embracing and commemorating death.

9. Bridging Life and Death:

Calaveras serve as a bridge between the realms of the living and the deceased. The imagery and use of calaveras help create a connection between the two worlds during the Day of the Dead.

10. The Cycle of Life and Death:

Calaveras symbolize the cyclical nature of life and death. They represent the idea that death is not an end but a part of the ongoing journey, reinforcing the celebration of life within the context of mortality.

Calaveras, with their rich history and symbolism, are an essential and vibrant part of the Day of the Dead celebration. They capture the essence of how the holiday blends humor, art, remembrance, and cultural heritage to commemorate the

departed and embrace the cycle of life and
death.

Chapter Ten: Modern Interpretations and Changes

Modern interpretations and changes in the celebration of the Day of the Dead (Día de los Muertos) have evolved in response to contemporary influences and global awareness. While the core traditions and symbolism of the holiday remain intact, there have been various shifts and adaptations. Here are some examples of modern interpretations and changes in the celebration:

1. Global Awareness and Popularity:

The Day of the Dead has gained global recognition and popularity. Many people outside of Mexico now celebrate and appreciate the holiday, leading to cross-cultural influences and adaptations.

2. Artistic Expression:

Contemporary artists have played a significant role in reimagining and expanding the artistic aspects of the celebration. From contemporary art exhibitions to multimedia installations, the artistic interpretations of the Day of the Dead have evolved.

3. Commercialization:

The holiday has seen commercial influences, with the sale of Day of the Dead-themed merchandise and products. This has led to a broader awareness of the celebration but also concerns about cultural appropriation.

4. Social Media and Pop Culture:

The prevalence of social media and pop culture has brought Day of the Dead into mainstream awareness. It's now a common theme in films, TV shows, and advertising campaigns.

5. Interfaith and Inter-Cultural Dialogue:

Interfaith and inter-cultural dialogues have shaped the way Day of the Dead is celebrated by individuals from diverse backgrounds. People of various religious and cultural backgrounds may incorporate elements of the celebration into their own practices.

6. Personalization and Creativity:

Many individuals and communities have personalized the Day of the Dead to reflect their own experiences and beliefs. They may incorporate new elements, themes, or artistic expressions into their celebrations.

7. Environmental Consciousness:

Some contemporary adaptations include a focus on environmental sustainability. Efforts are made to reduce waste and minimize the environmental impact of the celebration, such as using biodegradable materials for ofrendas and decorations.

8. Expanded Meaning and Inclusivity:

Some contemporary celebrations seek to broaden the Day of the Dead's meaning to encompass various aspects of remembrance, including commemorating social justice movements, honoring deceased pets, or addressing current global issues.

9. Diaspora Communities:

Mexican diaspora communities around the world have adapted the Day of the Dead to their local environments while retaining its core traditions. This has resulted in unique variations of the celebration in different countries.

10. Cultural Exchange:

International cultural exchange programs and festivals have contributed to a sharing of traditions. Mexican communities abroad often host Day of the Dead events to share their culture with others.

These contemporary adaptations and influences reflect the dynamic nature of culture and how traditions can evolve while retaining their core values. The Day of the Dead continues to be a meaningful and vibrant celebration that bridges the past with the present and transcends cultural boundaries. It exemplifies how a cultural celebration can be both rooted in tradition and open to interpretation, making it relevant and significant in today's world.

How the celebration has evolved over time

The celebration of the Day of the Dead (Día de los Muertos) has evolved over time through a complex interplay of historical, cultural, and social influences. While the core elements of the holiday have remained intact, several significant changes and developments have taken place. Here's how the celebration has evolved over time:

1. Indigenous Roots:

The origins of the celebration can be traced back to indigenous Mesoamerican cultures, including the Aztecs and Maya. These civilizations had their own death-related rituals and beliefs, which merged with Catholicism during the Spanish colonization.

2. Spanish Influence:

With the arrival of the Spanish conquistadors in the 16th century, indigenous traditions and Catholicism became intertwined. The celebration of All Saints' Day (Día de Todos los Santos) on November 1st and All Souls' Day (Día de los Fieles Difuntos) on November 2nd merged with indigenous traditions to create the modern Day of the Dead.

3. Blend of Beliefs:

The Day of the Dead combines indigenous beliefs in the cyclical nature of life and death with Catholic teachings on the afterlife, heaven, and purgatory. This blend of beliefs is reflected in the various rituals and symbolism of the holiday.

4. Regional Variations:

Different regions of Mexico have developed their own unique traditions and customs related to the Day of the Dead. These regional variations are influenced by local cultures and history, resulting in a diverse tapestry of practices.

5. Artistic Expression:

The celebration has always had strong artistic elements, from intricate sugar skulls to papel picado (cut paper) decorations. Over time, these artistic expressions have become more elaborate and creative, with artists and artisans incorporating new materials and techniques.

6. Commercialization:

In recent decades, the Day of the Dead has seen commercial influences, with the sale of themed merchandise, decorations, and products. This has both increased global awareness of the holiday and raised concerns about cultural appropriation.

7. Global Awareness:

The Day of the Dead has gained international recognition and is celebrated by people around the world. Its symbolism and aesthetics have been embraced in diverse cultural contexts.

8. Environmental Consciousness:

In response to environmental concerns, there is a growing emphasis on sustainability in the celebration. Biodegradable materials and eco-friendly practices are encouraged to minimize the environmental impact.

9. Personalization and Inclusivity:

Many individuals and communities personalize the celebration to reflect their own experiences and beliefs. The holiday is also becoming more inclusive, with some celebrations recognizing and commemorating a broader range of deceased individuals and issues.

10. Preservation of Tradition:

Despite the changes and adaptations, there is a strong commitment to preserving the core values and traditions of the Day of the Dead. Families and communities continue to honor and remember their deceased loved ones through ofrendas, visits to cemeteries, and other traditional practices.

The evolution of the Day of the Dead reflects its resilience and adaptability, as it continues to be a vibrant and meaningful celebration that bridges the past with the present. It serves as a testament to the enduring connection between the living and the deceased and the importance of cultural heritage in contemporary society.

Influence of tourism and globalization

The celebration of the Day of the Dead has been significantly influenced by tourism and globalization. These influences have brought both opportunities and challenges to the traditional practices and customs associated with the holiday. Here's an exploration of how tourism and globalization have impacted the Day of the Dead:

Positive Influences:

1. Increased Awareness:

Tourism and globalization have led to increased global awareness of the Day of the Dead. People from around the world have come to learn about and appreciate this unique Mexican tradition.

2. Economic Opportunities:

The influx of tourists during the Day of the Dead has created economic opportunities for local communities. Artisans, food vendors, and local businesses benefit from the boost in tourism.

3. Cultural Exchange:

The holiday has become a platform for cultural exchange. International visitors and artists sometimes participate in or learn about the Day of the Dead, promoting cross-cultural understanding and appreciation.

4. Revitalization and Preservation:

In some cases, the international interest in the Day of the Dead has motivated local communities to revitalize and preserve their traditions. This includes the restoration of cemeteries and the continuation of ancestral practices.

5. Creativity and Innovation:

The globalization of the Day of the Dead has encouraged creativity and innovation. New artistic expressions and adaptations have emerged, enriching the celebration.

Challenges and Concerns:

1. Commercialization:

The commercialization of the Day of the Dead, with the sale of themed merchandise and products, has raised concerns about cultural appropriation. The commercial aspect can sometimes overshadow the cultural and spiritual significance of the holiday.

2. Loss of Authenticity:

There is a concern that the influx of tourists and international interest in the Day of the Dead may lead to the dilution or loss of the holiday's authentic and traditional elements.

3. Cultural Misinterpretation:

Cultural misunderstandings or misinterpretations can occur when international visitors do not fully grasp the nuances and depth of the holiday's symbolism and practices.

4. Environmental Impact:

The growing number of tourists and the use of non-biodegradable materials for decorations can have negative environmental consequences, such as waste and pollution.

5. Impact on Local Communities:

In some popular tourist destinations, the surge in visitors during the Day of the Dead can put a strain on local infrastructure, disrupt daily life, and displace local residents.

Balancing Act:

Communities and authorities often face the challenge of striking a balance between accommodating tourists and preserving the authenticity and cultural significance of the Day of the Dead. Strategies to achieve this balance include responsible tourism practices, cultural education, and regulations on commercial activities.

In conclusion, tourism and globalization have brought both positive and negative influences to the celebration of the Day of the Dead. While these forces have increased awareness and provided economic opportunities, they have also raised concerns about cultural appropriation, authenticity, and sustainability. Communities and authorities are continually working to navigate these influences while preserving the cultural richness and spirituality of the holiday.

Controversies and challenges faced by the tradition

The celebration of the Day of the Dead (Día de los Muertos) faces several controversies and challenges, some of which are inherent to the evolving nature of the tradition, while others are related to social, cultural, and environmental factors. Here are some of the key controversies and challenges faced by the tradition:

1. Commercialization:

The commercialization of the Day of the Dead has raised concerns about cultural appropriation and the commodification of a sacred tradition. The sale of themed merchandise, decorations, and products sometimes overshadows the holiday's cultural and spiritual significance.

2. Cultural Appropriation:

As the celebration gains global popularity, there is a risk of cultural appropriation, where elements of the Day of the Dead are used out of context or without understanding their significance. Misinterpretation and misuse of symbols can be offensive to the communities that observe the tradition.

3. Authenticity:

The increasing popularity of the Day of the Dead, both in Mexico and internationally, has led to concerns about the preservation of its authenticity. There is a fear that the holiday's traditional elements may be diluted or altered to cater to commercial interests or outside influences.

4. Environmental Impact:

The use of non-biodegradable materials in decorations, such as plastic and synthetic materials, has raised environmental concerns. The waste generated during the holiday can have a negative impact on the environment, including pollution and litter.

5. Tourist Overload:

In popular tourist destinations, the Day of the Dead can attract an overwhelming number of visitors, leading to overcrowding, strain on local infrastructure, and disruption of local residents' lives.

6. Ethical Concerns:

In some cases, there have been ethical concerns regarding the involvement of international tourists in the celebration, including issues related to respect for local traditions and practices.

7. Cultural Misunderstanding:

Cultural misunderstandings can arise when international visitors do not fully comprehend the cultural and spiritual significance of the holiday. This can lead to insensitivity or misinterpretation of rituals and symbols.

8. Preservation of Indigenous Languages:

Some indigenous communities that celebrate the Day of the Dead are struggling to preserve their native languages, which are essential for understanding the oral traditions and rituals associated with the holiday.

9. Urbanization:

The migration of rural populations to urban areas in Mexico has led to a disconnection from ancestral lands and traditions, affecting the way the Day of the Dead is celebrated. Many people now observe the holiday in more urbanized and contemporary contexts.

10. Generational Changes:

Younger generations may not always have the same level of interest or understanding of the Day of the Dead as their elders, which can impact the transmission of cultural knowledge and traditions.

Addressing these controversies and challenges requires a delicate balance between preserving the authentic elements of the Day of the Dead while allowing for cultural exchange and adaptation. Communities, cultural organizations, and authorities work to develop responsible tourism practices, promote cultural education, and establish regulations to ensure the holiday's cultural and spiritual significance remains intact.

Made in United States
Troutdale, OR
08/08/2024